NEW FIRST STEPS
IN LATIN

NEW FIRST STEPS IN LATIN

Lee Pearcy
Mary Allen
Thomas Kent
Michael Klaassen
Mary Van Dyke Konopka
Alexander Pearson

Department of Classical Languages
The Episcopal Academy

Focus Publishing
Newburyport, Massachusetts

ISBN 1-58510-008-0

10 9 8 7 6 5

Printed in Canada

PREFACE

New First Steps in Latin is grounded in pedagogical practice. It is based on an old idea, that learning Latin plays an important role in the cognitive development of all young adolescents. It is based on a new idea, that learning Latin by the grammar-translation method can help students who process language in non-standard ways to become aware of language and their own use of it.

In 1995-96, two members of The Episcopal Academy's Classics Department team-taught an eighth-grade Latin class. Several students in the class were finding it hard to learn Latin, and the two teachers worked with them individually and in small groups, all the time trying to identify the sources of their difficulties. All six members of the department became drawn into this intriguing pedagogical problem.

Working together and with our students, we discovered that many of the students had identifiable learning differences. They experienced great difficulty with the layout and presentation of their textbook, an in-house reprint of Francis Ritchie's *Second Steps in Latin*, which was first published in 1898 and issued in revised editions until 1978. The textbook's age was not the problem. Ritchie's venerable text, along with his *First Steps in Latin*, was still the best textbook that we could find for our middle schoolers. We had tried or evaluated the others, and they did not work in our classrooms.

From this experience, and from dozens of conversations and classroom experiments, has come *New First Steps in Latin*. In the summer of 1998, with the support of Episcopal's Class of 1944 Fund and Parents' Association, we spent six weeks working full-time on Phase I of this project. We prepared a draft of *New First Steps in Latin*, began work on the Internet-based version of this text and its teachers' manual, and began investigations that will ground our pedagogical intuitions in modern work on cognitive processes and learning styles. During the 1998-99 school year a draft was tested with one section of middle-school beginners, and work continued, again with support from Episcopal's Class of 1944, during the summer of 1999. We hope to follow *New First Steps* with *New Second Steps*, a teachers' manual, Internet-based instructional material, and other instructional tools.

It is a pleasure for us to thank here some of those who have made this book possible. Episcopal Academy's Class of 1944, and in particular H. Alan Hume, Bruce Mainwaring, and Newbold Smith, led the way in supporting our work on this book. Jay Crawford, Randy Woods, Jon Kulp, and other members of Episcopal's administration encouraged us to turn our ideas into print and practice and gave us the freedom to do so. Ron Pullins and his staff at Focus Publishing encouraged us along the way and turned our computer files into a book. Finally, through their energy, enthusiasm, and eagerness to learn, our students in Episcopal Academy's Middle and Upper Schools have contributed more to this book than they may know.

The Episcopal Academy Classics Department
Lee Pearcy, Mary Allen,
Tim Kent, Michael Klaassen,
Molly Konopka, Alex Pearson

INTRODUCTION
To the Student

Why study Latin? Latin is the language of the ancient Romans, and of the people who have based important parts of their cultures on them. The first reason to study Latin, then, is because knowing it is the best way to know about these important peoples and their histories.

By studying Latin, you will also learn how to think and talk about language in general. You will learn many grammatical terms that apply to other languages as well as to Latin. By analyzing the structure of Latin sentences, you will train your mind to think logically and you will understand your own language better. You will learn to pay attention to detail and to be precise; in Latin every letter can make a difference. These are skills that will serve you well in everything you will do.

You will also train your memory. Nothing you learn in the beginning is unnecessary later. You will build constantly on what you learned earlier, and what you learn this year will be the foundation for next year's work.

Many English words have developed from Latin roots. Very soon you will find that you have become better at deciphering the meaning of unfamiliar English words.

We encourage you to bring energy and enthusiasm to the study of Latin. Be conscientious, organized, and precise. Although we cannot promise you that learning Latin will be easy, we can promise you it will be both constructive and rewarding.

CONTENTS
Lessons

Appendix

Lesson I

VERBS

VERBS have person, number, tense, mood, and voice.

The **PERSON** is 1st, 2nd, or 3rd: **NUMBER** is singular or plural :

SINGULAR		PLURAL	
1st person	*I*	1st person	*we*
2nd person	*you*	2nd person	*you*
3rd person	*he, she, it*	3rd person	*they*

There are six **TENSES**: present, imperfect, future, perfect, pluperfect, future perfect.

There are five **MOODS**: indicative, subjunctive, imperative, infinitive, participle.

There are two **VOICES**: active, passive.

FIRST CONJUGATION: Ā-VERBS
Present System Active Voice

There are four categories of verbs in Latin, known as **CONJUGATIONS**.

A verb has four **PRINCIPAL PARTS**.

   Example: **amō, amāre, amāvī, amātum**

Verbs whose second principal part ends in **-āre** belong to the **FIRST CONJUGATION**.

To find the present stem of a First Conjugation verb, remove **-re** from the second principal part.

$$\begin{array}{r} \text{AMĀRE} \\ \underline{- \text{ RE}} \\ \text{AMĀ-} \end{array}$$

The **PRESENT** tense is formed by adding the personal endings to the present stem: **amā -**

PRESENT TENSE

Singular	personal endings		present stem + personal ending			
1st person	**-ō**	→	am**ō***	*I love,*	*- am loving,*	*- do love*
2nd person	**-s**	→	am**ā**s	*you love,*	*- are loving,*	*- do love*
3rd person	**-t**	→	ama**t**	*he/she/it loves,*	*- is loving,*	*- does love*
Plural						
1st person	**-mus**	→	amā**mus**	*we love,*	*- are loving,*	*- do love*
2nd person	**-tis**	→	amā**tis**	*you love,*	*- are loving,*	*- do love*
3rd person	**-nt**	→	ama**nt**	*they love,*	*- are loving,*	*- do love*

*The stem vowel -ā- is dropped in front of the first person singular ending, -ō.

- Note that there are three ways to express the present tense in English.

In Latin the personal ending is usually used instead of the personal pronoun to indicate the subject; therefore the word **amat** may be a complete sentence, *He loves.*

Vocabulary I

1st Conjugation Verbs (like **amō**)					Adverb	
I	II	III	IV			
amō,	amāre,	amāvī,	amātum	*love, like*	nōn	*not*
laudō,	laudāre,	laudāvī,	laudātum	*praise*		
rogō,	rogāre,	rogāvī,	rogātum	*ask*		
vocō,	vocāre,	vocāvī,	vocātum	*call*		
vulnerō,	vulnerāre,	vulnerāvī,	vulnerātum	*wound, hurt*		

Exercise I

A.

1. Amāmus.
2. Rogant.
3. Vocās.
4. Vulnerō.
5. Laudat.
6. Vulnerātis.
7. Vocant.
8. Nōn laudō.
9. Rogat.
10. Amant.
11. Nōn laudātis.
12. Nōn vulnerant.
13. Amat.
14. Rogāmus.
15. Nōn vocō.
16. Amās.
17. Laudant.
18. Vulnerās.
19. Amātis.
20. Nōn vocāmus.

B.

1. I praise.
2. We are calling.
3. You (sg.) love.
4. He does not ask.
5. They wound.
6. You (pl.) love.
7. It is wounding.
8. I am praising.
9. You (pl.) do not call.
10. We praise.
11. She is praising.
12. They do wound.
13. I call.
14. You (pl.) are asking.
15. We love.
16. He loves.
17. You (sg.) ask.
18. They are not calling.
19. We are wounding.
20. It is not praising.

Lesson II

FIRST CONJUGATION: Ā-VERBS
Present System Active Voice

The **IMPERFECT** tense expresses continuous or repeated action in past time. The letters **-bā-** appear before the personal endings:

IMPERFECT TENSE

Singular	imperfect endings		present stem + ending			
1st person	-bam	→	amābam	*I was loving,*	*- loved,*	*- used to love*
2nd person	-bās	→	amābās	*you were loving,*	*- loved,*	*- used to love*
3rd person	-bat	→	amabat	*he/she/it was loving,*	*- loved,*	*- used to love*
Plural						
1st person	-bāmus	→	amābāmus	*we were loving,*	*- loved,*	*- used to love*
2nd person	-bātis	→	amābātis	*you were loving,*	*- loved,*	*- used to love*
3rd person	-bant	→	amabant	*they were loving,*	*- loved,*	*- used to love*

- There are various ways to express the imperfect tense in English: I <u>was loving</u>, I <u>loved</u>, I <u>used to love</u>.

The **FUTURE** tense expresses action yet to happen. First Conjugation verbs use the letter **-b-** + variable vowel before adding the personal endings.

FUTURE TENSE

Singular	future endings		present stem + ending		
1st person	-bō	→	amābō	*I will love,*	*- am going to love*
2nd person	-bis	→	amābis	*you will love,*	*- are going to love*
3rd person	-bit	→	amabit	*he/she/it will love,*	*- is going to love*
Plural					
1st person	-bimus	→	amābimus	*we will love,*	*- are going to love*
2nd person	-bitis	→	amābitis	*you will love,*	*- are going to love*
3rd person	-bunt	→	amabunt	*they will love,*	*- are going to love*

Vocabulary II

1st Conjugation Verbs (like **amō**)				
cantō,	cantāre,	cantāvī,	cantātum	*sing*
errō,	errāre,	errāvī,	errātum	*wander; be mistaken*
portō,	portāre,	portāvī,	portātum	*carry*
pugnō,	pugnāre,	pugnāvī,	pugnātum	*fight*

Exercise II

A.

1. Laudāmus.
2. Vocābit.
3. Pugnābant.
4. Vulnerābitis.
5. Cantās.
6. Rogō.
7. Amābam.
8. Errat.
9. Nōn vocant.
10. Nōn portābās.
11. Cantābō.
12. Nōn rogābat.
13. Nōn portābimus.
14. Amābunt.
15. Errābātis.
16. Nōn errābit.
17. Laudant.
18. Vocābam.
19. Nōn vulnerābant.
20. Pugnābimus.

B.

1. He used to wound.
2. They were fighting.
3. You (sg.) will love.
4. I will sing.
5. You (pl.) were praising.
6. It will carry.
7. I was not asking.
8. She is going to like.
9. You (pl.) are mistaken.
10. They do not sing.
11. They will ask.
12. I am going to wander.
13. She is fighting.
14. You (pl.) were calling.
15. You (sg.) were wounding.
16. We will not be mistaken.
17. He used to wander.
18. I am going to praise.
19. We used to love.
20. We will not carry.

Lesson III

FIRST CONJUGATION: Ā-VERBS
Perfect System Active Voice

The **PERFECT** tense expresses completed action in past time.

The **PERFECT STEM** is found by removing the final **-ī** from the third principal part: **AMĀVĪ**.

$$\begin{array}{r} \text{AMĀVĪ} \\ \underline{\quad -\bar{\text{I}}\quad} \\ \text{AMĀV-} \end{array}$$

The perfect tense is formed by adding the perfect endings to the perfect stem.

PERFECT TENSE

Singular	perfect endings		perfect stem + ending			
1st person	-ī	→	amāvī	*I loved,*	*- have loved,*	*- did love*
2nd person	-istī	→	amāvistī	*you loved,*	*- have loved,*	*- did love*
3rd person	-it	→	amavit	*he/she/it loved,*	*- has loved,*	*- did love*
Plural						
1st person	-imus	→	amāvimus	*we loved,*	*- have loved,*	*- did love*
2nd person	-istis	→	amāvistis	*you loved,*	*- have loved,*	*- did love*
3rd person	-ērunt	→	amavērunt	*they loved,*	*- have loved,*	*- did love*

Learn to recognize and use distinct translations of the perfect tense:

Aorist translation

I loved,	*- did love*	*we loved,*	*- did love*
you loved,	*- did love*	*you loved,*	*- did love*
he/she/it loved,	*- did love*	*they loved,*	*- did love*

Perfect translation

I have loved	*we have loved*
you have loved	*you have loved*
he/she/it has loved	*they have loved*

Vocabulary III

1st Conjugation Verbs (like **amō**)					Conjunction	
servō,	servāre,	servāvī,	servātum	*watch over, guard, save*	et	*and*
parō,	parāre,	parāvī,	parātum	*prepare*		

Exercise III

A.

1. Cantāvī.
2. Parāvērunt.
3. Rogāvistis.
4. Pugnāvistī.
5. Vocāvimus et laudāvimus.
6. Nōn servābat.
7. Nōn errāvērunt.
8. Laudāvit et amāvērunt.
9. Amās.
10. Parāvit.
11. Nōn portābat.
12. Vulnerāvī.
13. Pugnāvērunt.
14. Laudābis.
15. Nōn amābāmus.
16. Parāvī et servāvī.
17. Servās.
18. Vulnerāvit.
19. Parābunt.
20. Nōn portābit.
21. Errāvistis.
22. Parāvimus et servāvimus.
23. Nōn rogābō.
24. Cantābam.

B.

1. I have prepared.
2. He did wound.
3. We saved.
4. You (pl.) sang.
5. You (sg.) were praising.
6. They have carried.
7. It has not called.
8. I will watch over.
9. She was loving.
10. I am asking.
11. They have not praised.
12. You (sg.) wandered.
13. We have asked.
14. You (sg.) used to prepare.
15. I fought.
16. They will call and you (pl.) will save.
17. She is wandering.
18. You (pl.) have guarded.
19. I will not hurt.
20. He was singing.
21. We will prepare and we will carry.
22. They have not loved.
23. She has saved.
24. You (sg.) have not asked.

Lesson IV

FIRST CONJUGATION: Ā-VERBS
Perfect System Active Voice

THE PLUPERFECT TENSE is formed by adding the pluperfect endings to the perfect stem. The pluperfect endings include the letters **-erā-** before the personal endings.

PLUPERFECT TENSE

Singular	pluperfect endings		perfect stem + ending	
1st person	-eram	→	amāveram	*I had loved*
2nd person	-erās	→	amāverās	*you had loved*
3rd person	-erat	→	amaverat	*he/she/it had loved*
Plural				
1st person	-erāmus	→	amāverāmus	*we had loved*
2nd person	-erātis	→	amāverātis	*you had loved*
3rd person	-erant	→	amaverant	*they had loved*

- The pluperfect tense is translated with the helping verb *had*.

THE FUTURE PERFECT TENSE is formed by adding the future perfect endings to the perfect stem. The future perfect endings include the letters **-eri-** before the personal endings. In the first person singular, the ending is **-erō**.

FUTURE PERFECT TENSE

Singular	future perfect endings		perfect stem + ending	
1st person	-erō	→	amāverō	*I will have loved*
2nd person	-eris	→	amāveris	*you will have loved*
3rd person	-erit	→	amaverit	*he/she/it will have loved*
Plural				
1st person	-erimus	→	amāverimus	*we will have loved*
2nd person	-eritis	→	amāveritis	*you will have loved*
3rd person	-erint	→	amaverint	*they will have loved*

- The future perfect tense is translated with the helping verb *will have*.

THE SENTENCE

Every **SENTENCE** consists of a **SUBJECT** and a **PREDICATE**.

The subject is what the sentence is about.   The predicate is what is said about the subject.

In Latin, a sentence can consist of a single word:

Example: <u>Amat</u>. *She loves.*   (The subject is expressed by the personal ending of the verb.)

OR the subject may be a separate word in the **NOMINATIVE CASE**.

Example: <u>Puella</u> amat.   *The <u>girl</u> loves.*

8

Vocabulary IV

<table>
<tr><td colspan="4">1st Declension Nouns</td></tr>
<tr><td>Nominative</td><td>Genitive</td><td>Gender</td><td></td></tr>
<tr><td>puella,</td><td>puellae,</td><td>feminine</td><td>*girl*</td></tr>
<tr><td>rēgīna,</td><td>rēgīnae,</td><td>feminine</td><td>*queen*</td></tr>
<tr><td>agricola,</td><td>agricolae,</td><td>masculine</td><td>*farmer*</td></tr>
<tr><td>poēta,</td><td>poētae,</td><td>masculine</td><td>*poet*</td></tr>
</table>

- Nouns will always be introduced in the manner above: The nominative, genitive, gender and English meaning.

Exercise IV

A.

1. Parāverās.
2. Laudāverant.
3. Laudābās.
4. Amāverimus.
5. Nōn vulnerāverāmus.
6. Cantāveram.
7. Pugnāveritis et vulnerāveritis.
8. Errābunt.
9. Rēgīna vocāverit.
10. Puella rogāvit.
11. Vocābit et rogābit.
12. Nōn portāverant.
13. Poēta cantāvit.
14. Agricola errat et cantat.
15. Puella nōn rogāverat.
16. Agricola portat.
17. Nōn amāverātis.
18. Servāverō.
19. Nōn vulnerāvistī.
20. Rēgīna nōn pugnāverit.

B.

1. You (pl.) will have sung.
2. We had prepared.
3. She had not sung.
4. You (sg.) will have carried.
5. He had not praised.
6. The girl will have been mistaken.
7. You (sg.) are guarding.
8. We had loved.
9. The poet was praising.
10. They had called.
11. I had fought and wandered.
12. The queen will ask.
13. The farmer will have asked.
14. We were not calling.
15. I am mistaken.
16. The farmer has fought.
17. You (sg.) have prepared.
18. You (pl.) had not wounded.
19. They had saved.
20. The girl was liking.

Lesson V

FIRST DECLENSION NOUNS

NOUNS have case, number, and gender.

There are five **CASES**: nominative, genitive, dative, accusative, ablative.

There are two **NUMBERS**: singular, plural.

There are three **GENDERS**: masculine, feminine, neuter.

Nouns of the first declension have a genitive singular ending in **–ae**.

To find the stem of any Latin noun remove the ending from the genitive singular form:

PUELLAE
_____ -AE
PUELL-

Nouns are declined by adding case endings to the noun stem.

Singular	1ˢᵗ declension endings		stem + ending	
Nominative	-a	→	puella	*the girl*
Genitive	-ae	→	puellae	*of the girl, girl's*
Dative	-ae	→	puellae	*to / for the girl*
Accusative	-am	→	puellam	*the girl*
Ablative	-ā	→	puellā	*by / with / from the girl*
Plural				
Nominative	-ae	→	puellae	*girls*
Genitive	-ārum	→	puellārum	*of the girls, girls'*
Dative	-īs	→	puellīs	*to / for the girls*
Accusative	-ās	→	puellās	*girls*
Ablative	-īs	→	puellīs	*by / with / from the girls*

Latin has no **ARTICLES**. Supply the **DEFINITE ARTICLE** *the* or the **INDEFINITE ARTICLE** *a / an* as needed in English.

Most nouns of the first declension are of the feminine gender.

RULE: The subject of a sentence is in the nominative case.

    Example: Puella (nom.) cantat.   *The girl sings.*

RULE: The Verb agrees with its subject in person and number. This is the **FIRST RULE OF CONCORD**.

    Examples: Puella (3ʳᵈ sg.) cantat (3ʳᵈ sg.).   *The girl sings.*
                      Puellae (3ʳᵈ pl.) cantant (3ʳᵈ pl.).   *The girls sing.*

Vocabulary V

1st Declension Nouns (like **puella**)			
Nominative	Genitive		
aqua,	aquae,	f.	*water*
epistula,	epistulae,	f.	*letter*
patria,	patriae,	f.	*native land*

- From now on the gender will always be abbreviated: m. = masculine, f. = feminine, and n. = neuter.

Exercise V

A.

1. Rēgīna pugnat.
2. Puellae nōn errābant.
3. Rēgīna vulnerābit.
4. Poēta nōn errābit.
5. Aquae cantābant.
6. Patria laudāverat.
7. Portābis.
8. Nōn rogō.
9. Agricola servāverit.
10. Rēgīnae portāverant.
11. Poētae cantant.
12. Vocāvistis.
13. Nōn portābimus.
14. Puella laudāverat et rogāvit.
15. Agricolae et poētae nōn pugnant.
16. Epistulae nōn laudāverint.
17. Puellae cantāvērunt.
18. Parāvistī.
19. Agricolae servāverant.
20. Nōn vulnerāveram.

B.

1. He is singing.
2. You (pl.) did hurt.
3. I was preparing.
4. The farmer has sung.
5. The girls did not ask.
6. The queen prepares.
7. The poets will have praised.
8. A girl loves and sings.
9. We will have watched over.
10. The poets wander.
11. The girls will have fought.
12. The native land was calling.
13. They are not carrying.
14. I had fought and wounded.
15. The farmer used to call and ask.
16. The letter will praise.
17. The queen sang.
18. You (pl.) had been mistaken.
19. We had called and praised.
20. The farmer has not called.

Lesson VI

SECOND CONJUGATION: -Ē VERBS
Present System Active Voice

Verbs whose second principal part ends in **-ēre** belong to the **SECOND CONJUGATION**:

Example: **moneō, monēre, monuī, monitum**

To find the present stem of a second conjugation verb, remove the **-re** from the second principal part.

$$\frac{\text{MONĒRE}}{\text{MONĒ-}} \quad \text{-RE}$$

The **-ē-** of the stem shortens before another vowel and before final **-t** or **-nt**.

PRESENT TENSE

Singular	present stem + ending			
1st person	mone**ō**	*I advise,*	*- am advising,*	*- do advise*
2nd person	mon**ēs**	*you advise,*	*- are advising,*	*- do advise*
3rd person	mone**t**	*he/she/it advises,*	*- is advising,*	*- does advise*
Plural				
1st person	mon**ēmus**	*we advise,*	*- are advising,*	*- do advise*
2nd person	mon**ētis**	*you advise,*	*- are advising,*	*- do advise*
3rd person	mone**nt**	*they advise,*	*- are advising,*	*- do advise*

IMPERFECT TENSE

Singular	present stem + ending			
1st person	monē**bam**	*I was advising,*	*- advised,*	*- used to advise*
2nd person	monē**bās**	*you were advising,*	*- advised,*	*- used to advise*
3rd person	monē**bat**	*he/she/it was advising,*	*- advised,*	*- used to advise*
Plural				
1st person	monē**bāmus**	*we were advising,*	*- advised,*	*- used to advise*
2nd person	monē**bātis**	*you were advising,*	*- advised,*	*- used to advise*
3rd person	mone**bant**	*they were advising,*	*- advised,*	*- used to advise*

FUTURE TENSE

Singular	present stem + ending		
1st person	monē**bō**	*I will advise,*	*- am going to advise*
2nd person	monē**bis**	*you will advise,*	*- are going to advise*
3rd person	monē**bit**	*he/she/it will advise,*	*- is going to advise*
Plural			
1st person	monē**bimus**	*we will advise,*	*- are going to advise*
2nd person	monē**bitis**	*you will advise,*	*- are going to advise*
3rd person	mone**bunt**	*they will advise,*	*- are going to advise*

DIRECT OBJECTS OF TRANSITIVE VERBS

A noun that receives the action of a verb is a **DIRECT OBJECT**. A verb which takes a direct object is called **TRANSITIVE**.

RULE: The direct object of a transitive verb is in the accusative case. In a Latin sentence, the direct object usually comes before the verb:

Magister <u>puellam</u> laudat.   *The teacher praises the girl.*

"Girl" is the direct object of the transitive verb "praises." **Puellam**, in the accusative, is the direct object of the transitive verb **laudat**.

Vocabulary VI

2nd Conjugation Verbs (like **moneō**)					Conjunction	
moneō,	monēre,	monuī,	monitum	*warn, advise*	sed	*but*
terreō,	terrēre,	terruī,	territum	*frighten*		
doceō,	docēre,	docuī,	doctum	*teach*		
teneō,	tenēre,	tenuī,	tentum	*hold, contain*		

Exercise VI

A.

1. Puella rēgīnam docet.
2. Agricola aquam tenēbat.
3. Aqua puellam terret.
4. Agricola patriam amat.
5. Poēta rēgīnam monēbit.
6. Epistulam servāverātis, sed errāvistis.
7. Nōn cantābimus, sed docēbimus.
8. Agricolās terrēbātis.
9. Puellae epistulam parābant.
10. Puellae patriam amāverint.
11. Puellae nōn cantāvērunt.
12. Poētae rēgīnam laudāvērunt.
13. Agricolae aquam nōn tenent.
14. Poētae nōn pugnābant sed rēgīnam monēbant.
15. Poēta epistulam parābit et rēgīnam docēbit.
16. Poētae agricolam vocābant et laudābant.
17. Rēgīna agricolās monēbat.
18. Puella rēgīnās monet et docet.
19. Poētae patriam servāvērunt.
20. Aquam laudātis.
21. Epistulam tenēbāmus.
22. Patriam amō.
23. Rēgīnam nōn laudāverāmus.
24. Epistulās tenēbunt.

B.

1. The queen teaches the girl.
2. The girls will advise the queen.
3. The queens were teaching the girls.
4. A girl frightened the farmer.
5. The water will frighten the poets.
6. We wounded the farmers.
7. You (pl.) were holding the letters.
8. I will teach the farmers.
9. He has not called the poet.
10. Poets sing and advise queens.
11. The girls were holding letters.
12. You (pl.) have hurt the poets.
13. The queen used to teach the poet.
14. The poets will teach the queen.
15. We will have carried the water.
16. You (sg.) advised the queen.
17. Girls love water, but farmers love the native land.
18. He was warning the farmer, but was frightening the girl.
19. You (sg.) had carried the letters, but you wandered.

Lesson VII

SECOND CONJUGATION: Ē-VERBS
Perfect System Active Voice

The **PERFECT STEM** is found by removing the final **-ī** from the third principal part: **monuī**.

$$\begin{array}{l} \text{MONUĪ} \\ \underline{\quad\quad -\bar{\imath}} \\ \text{MONU-} \end{array}$$

The perfect, pluperfect and future perfect tenses are formed by adding endings to the perfect stem.

- The endings are the same as in the first conjugation.

PERFECT TENSE

Singular	perfect stem + ending			
1st person	monuī	*I advised,*	*- have advised,*	*- did advise*
2nd person	monuistī	*you advised,*	*- have advised,*	*- did advise*
3rd person	monuit	*he/she/it advised,*	*- has advised,*	*- did advise*
Plural				
1st person	monuimus	*we advised,*	*- have advised,*	*- did advise*
2nd person	monuistis	*you advised,*	*- have advised,*	*- did advise*
3rd person	monuērunt	*they advised,*	*- have advised,*	*- did advise*

PLUPERFECT TENSE

Singular	perfect stem + ending	
1st person	monueram	*I had advised*
2nd person	monuerās	*you had advised*
3rd person	monuerat	*he/she/it had advised*
Plural		
1st person	monuerāmus	*we had advised*
2nd person	monuerātis	*you had advised*
3rd person	monuerant	*they had advised*

FUTURE PERFECT TENSE

Singular	perfect stem + ending	
1st person	monuero	*I will have advised*
2nd person	monueris	*you will have advised*
3rd person	monuerit	*he/she/it will have advised*
Plural		
1st person	monuerimus	*we will have advised*
2nd person	monueritis	*you will have advised*
3rd person	monuerint	*they will have advised*

GAPPING

A word having the same function in more than one clause need not be repeated in Latin.

Agricola umbram vīdit sed nōn puella.   *The farmer saw the ghost, but the girl did not.*

Sometimes the word used in both clauses appears only in the second.

Agricola umbram sed nōn puellam vīdit.   *The farmer saw the ghost, but not the girl.*

14

Vocabulary VII

2ⁿᵈ Conjugation Verbs (like **moneō**)					1ˢᵗ Declension Nouns (like **puella**)			
videō,	vidēre,	vīdī,	vīsum	*see*	īra,	īrae	f.	*anger, wrath*
					porta,	portae	f.	*gate*
					silva,	silvae	f.	*forest, woods*
					umbra,	umbrae	f.	*shadow, ghost*

Exercise VII

A.

1. Umbrae poētās terruērunt, sed nōn agricolās.
2. Umbrae agricolās terruērunt, sed nōn silvae.
3. Portās nōn vidēs, sed aquam.
4. Agricola poētam vīdit, sed nōn poēta agricolam.
5. Umbram nōn vīderās, sed vīderam.
6. Īram nōn amābam; īra puellam terruit.
7. Puella patriam vīderat, sed nōn aquam.
8. Portās nōn vidēbāmus, sed silvās.
9. Silvās amāverāmus, sed nōn umbrās.
10. Poētam nōn amās, sed agricolam amās.
11. Umbrae puellās nōn vulnerāverint.
12. Patriam nōn amāvistis, et aquam vīdistis.
13. Umbrās et silvās vidētis.
14. Puellae silvās amant.
15. Silvās servābimus, sed nōn portās.
16. Portae puellās nōn tenent.
17. Agricolae nōn pugnāverant.
18. Īra rēgīnās docuit et agricolam monuit.
19. Poētae silvās et aquam laudant.
20. Epistulae rēgīnam monuērunt.

B.

1. The poet has saved the queen, but not the farmer.
2. The poet did not advise the farmer, but the queen did.
3. The girls had held the water, but not the letters.
4. The ghost had terrified the poet, but not the girls.
5. The poets did not frighten the farmers, but the girls did.
6. We had not seen the gates.
7. You (pl.) had seen the forest, not the gates.
8. We love the woods and the shadows.
9. The ghost calls the girl, but not the queen.
10. They saw the letters, but not the ghost.
11. I had held the water, but the queen did not.
12. You (sg.) were seeing the shadows.
13. The letter had advised the queen.
14. We love the water, but not the forest.
15. The poets do not praise the forest.
16. We will have taught the poets.
17. They have held the water.
18. You (pl.) will prepare the letters.
19. The ghost saw the girls, but the girls did not see the ghost.
20. The poet will have taught the queen; the farmer won't have.

Lesson VIII

SECOND DECLENSION NOUNS

Nouns whose genitive singular ends in -ī belong to the **SECOND DECLENSION.**

To find the stem of any Latin noun, remove the ending from the genitive singular form.

$$\begin{array}{cc} \text{DOMINĪ} & \text{LIBRĪ} \\ \underline{\text{-ī}} & \underline{\text{-ī}} \\ \text{DOMIN-} & \text{LIBR-} \end{array}$$

- Masculine nouns of the second declension have a nominative singular ending in **-us** or **-r** .

Singular	2ⁿᵈ declension endings		stem + ending	
Nominative	-us	→	domin**us**	*the master*
Genitive	-ī	→	domin**ī**	*of the master, master's*
Dative	-ō	→	domin**ō**	*to / for the master*
Accusative	-um	→	domin**um**	*the master*
Ablative	-ō	→	domin**ō**	*by / with / from the master*
Plural				
Nominative	-ī	→	domin**ī**	*masters*
Genitive	-ōrum	→	domin**ōrum**	*of the masters, masters'*
Dative	-īs	→	domin**īs**	*to / for the masters*
Accusative	-ōs	→	domin**ōs**	*masters*
Ablative	-īs	→	domin**īs**	*by / with / from the masters*

Singular	2ⁿᵈ declension endings		stem + ending	
Nominative	—	→	liber	*the book*
Genitive	-ī	→	libr**ī**	*of the book, book's*
Dative	-ō	→	libr**ō**	*to / for the book*
Accusative	-um	→	libr**um**	*the book*
Ablative	-ō	→	libr**ō**	*by / with / from the book*
Plural				
Nominative	-ī	→	libr**ī**	*books*
Genitive	-ōrum	→	libr**ōrum**	*of the books, books'*
Dative	-īs	→	libr**īs**	*to / for the books*
Accusative	-ōs	→	libr**ōs**	*books*
Ablative	-īs	→	libr**īs**	*by / with / from the books*

- Note that in declining **liber** the -e- is dropped in all cases except nominative singular.

16

Vocabulary VIII

2nd Declension Nouns (like **liber** and **dominus**)							
ager,	agrī,	m.	*field*	dominus,	dominī,	m.	*master*
liber,	librī,	m.	*book*	deus,	deī,	m.	*god*
magister,	magistrī,	m.	*teacher*				

Exercise VIII

A.

1. Magister docuit.
2. Dominī librum tenēbunt.
3. Deī agricolam monuērunt.
4. Agricolae agrōs parāverint.
5. Liber dominum docuerit.
6. Aquam portāverāmus.
7. Silva umbrās nōn tenet.
8. Epistulās parābāmus, nōn librōs.
9. Deī et umbrae dominum terrēbant.
10. Rēgīna agrōs nōn laudat.
11. Agricola librōs et epistulās portābit.
12. Agricolae nōn errant, sed dominī.
13. Poēta nōn cantat.
14. Puellae deōs et agrōs vīdērunt.
15. Deōs monueram.
16. Nōn errāvistī.
17. Dominus portās servat.
18. Rēgīna poētās et magistrōs rogābit.
19. Liber īram laudāvit.
20. Agricolae pugnāverint, sed nōn poētae.
21. Umbra rēgīnās terruit, sed nōn magistrum.
22. Puellam vīdī et tenuī.
23. Puellae patriam amāverant, sed nōn rēgīnam.
24. Deī nōn pugnābant, et rēgīnam laudābant.

B.

1. A girl loves the book.
2. The teacher will have sung.
3. We will not advise the teacher.
4. The gods taught the girls, but not the master.
5. The book teaches the queens.
6. The letter had praised the master.
7. The god sees the native land and the queen.
8. I have called the god.
9. The queens were not wandering, but the ghosts were.
10. The book does not praise farmers.
11. The teacher will carry the girl.
12. The letters wound the poets.
13. I have held the letters.
14. You (pl.) had warned the farmers.
15. A book was praising the poet.
16. You (sg.) will see the gate.
17. I will ask the queen and the farmers.
18. Anger will have wounded the gods.
19. The teacher used to frighten the girls.
20. The farmer prepares the fields.
21. We saw the native land.
22. The books have not taught the girls, but the teacher has.
23. The queen will have sung.
24. Books warn the girls, but do not frighten (them).

Lesson IX

SECOND DECLENSION NOUNS *(continued)*

Second declension nouns ending in **–um** in the nominative singular are neuter.

Singular	2nd declension endings		stem + ending	
Nominative	**-um**	→	verb**um**	*the word*
Genitive	**-ī**	→	verb**ī**	*of the word, word's*
Dative	**-ō**	→	verb**ō**	*to / for the word*
Accusative	**-um**	→	verb**um**	*the word*
Ablative	**-ō**	→	verb**ō**	*by / with / from the word*
Plural				
Nominative	**-a**	→	verb**a**	*words*
Genitive	**-ōrum**	→	verb**ōrum**	*of the words, words'*
Dative	**-īs**	→	verb**īs**	*to / for the words*
Accusative	**-a**	→	verb**a**	*words*
Ablative	**-īs**	→	verb**īs**	*by / with / from the words*

RULE: For neuter nouns in Latin, the nominative and accusative forms are the same, and the plural of those cases ends in **–a**.

A few second declension masculine nouns have a stem that is the same as the nominative singular.

Singular		
Nominative	puer	*boy*
Genitive	puer**ī**	*of the boy, boy's*
Dative	puer**ō**	*to / for the boy*
Accusative	puer**um**	*boy*
Ablative	puer**ō**	*by / with / from the boy*
Plural		
Nominative	puer**ī**	*boys*
Genitive	puer**ōrum**	*of the boys, boys'*
Dative	puer**īs**	*to / for the boys*
Accusative	puer**ōs**	*boys*
Ablative	puer**īs**	*by / with / from the boys*

Vocabulary IX

2nd Conjugation Verbs (like **moneō**)	2nd Declension Nouns (like **verbum, magister**)			
timeō, timēre, timuī, — *fear, be afraid of*	factum,	factī,	n.	*deed*
	verbum,	verbī,	n.	*word*
	puer,	puerī,	m.	*boy*
	vir,	virī,	m.	*man*

Exercise IX

A.

1. Puer factum timet.
2. Magistrī verba docuerint.
3. Puerōs nōn timuerāmus.
4. Facta puerum docuērunt.
5. Factum puerōs terret.
6. Virōs vīderant, sed nōn umbrās.
7. Virī agrōs nōn servābunt.
8. Rēgīna verba cantābat.
9. Poētae umbrās vīdērunt, sed nōn silvās.
10. Rēgīna puerōs rogāvit.
11. Magistrī puerōs nōn monuērunt.
12. Rēgīna epistulās et librōs tenēbit.
13. Puellae et rēgīnae nōn pugnābant, sed cantābant.
14. Agricola agrōs parābat, poēta verba.
15. Librī virōs nōn terruērunt.
16. Vir verba nōn cantāverat.
17. Liber verba, nōn facta tenet.
18. Virī portās nōn servābunt.
19. Patriam nōn amāvistis, sed rēgīnam.
20. Nōn librōs, sed epistulās, teneō.

B.

1. I like the boy.
2. The girls prepare words.
3. The god will frighten the ghosts.
4. The man praises the native land, but not the queen.
5. The letter was holding words.
6. You (sg.) will have seen the deed.
7. The letters praise the girls.
8. The water had wandered.
9. We taught the deeds, but not the words.
10. The books have advised the boys.
11. The teacher was fearing the ghosts.
12. The masters will have called the god.
13. We had frightened the farmers, not the poet.
14. The gods will not carry the waters.
15. The boy had hurt the farmer.
16. The farmer did not prepare the field.
17. Anger will not wound the gods, but men.
18. You (pl.) were holding the gates.
19. I loved, but did not praise, the anger.
20. The gods praised the words and deeds.

Lesson X

THIRD CONJUGATION: CONSONANT VERBS
Present System Active Voice

Verbs whose second principal part ends in **-ere** belong to the **THIRD CONJUGATION**.
To find the present stem of a third conjugation verb, remove **-ere** from the second principal part.

Example: **dūcō, dūcere, dūxī, ductum** *lead*

$$\begin{array}{r} \text{DŪCERE} \\ \underline{\text{-ERE}} \\ \text{DŪC-} \end{array}$$

In the third conjugation a vowel appears between the stem and any ending beginning with a consonant. Note how the vowel varies.

PRESENT TENSE

Singular	endings		present stem + ending			
1ˢᵗ person	-ō	→	dūcō	*I lead,*	*- am leading,*	*- do lead*
2ⁿᵈ person	-s	→	dūcis	*you lead,*	*- are leading,*	*- do lead*
3ʳᵈ person	-t	→	dūcit	*he/she/it leads,*	*- is leading,*	*- does lead*
Plural						
1ˢᵗ person	-mus	→	dūcimus	*we lead,*	*- are leading,*	*- do lead*
2ⁿᵈ person	-tis	→	dūcitis	*you lead,*	*- are leading,*	*- do lead*
3ʳᵈ person	-nt	→	dūcunt	*they lead,*	*- are leading,*	*- do lead*

IMPERFECT TENSE

Singular	imperfect endings		present stem + ending			
1ˢᵗ person	-bam	→	dūcēbam	*I was leading,*	*- led,*	*- used to lead*
2ⁿᵈ person	-bās	→	dūcēbās	*you were leading,*	*- led,*	*- used to lead*
3ʳᵈ person	-bat	→	dūcēbat	*he/she/it was leading,*	*- led,*	*- used to lead*
Plural						
1ˢᵗ person	-bāmus	→	dūcēbāmus	*we were leading,*	*- led,*	*- used to lead*
2ⁿᵈ person	-bātis	→	dūcēbātis	*you were leading,*	*- led,*	*- used to lead*
3ʳᵈ person	-bant	→	dūcēbant	*they were leading,*	*- led,*	*- used to lead*

FUTURE TENSE

Singular	future endings		present stem + ending		
1ˢᵗ person	-am	→	dūcam	*I will lead,*	*- am going to lead*
2ⁿᵈ person	-ēs	→	dūcēs	*you will lead,*	*- are going to lead*
3ʳᵈ person	-et	→	dūcet	*he/she/it will lead,*	*- is going to lead*
Plural					
1ˢᵗ person	-ēmus	→	dūcēmus	*we will lead,*	*- are going to lead*
2ⁿᵈ person	-ētis	→	dūcētis	*you will lead,*	*- are going to lead*
3ʳᵈ person	-ent	→	dūcent	*they will lead,*	*- are going to lead*

- In the third conjugation the future tense is marked by vowels.

Vocabulary X

3rd Conjugation Verbs (like **dūcō**)				
dūcō,	dūcere,	dūxī,	ductum	*lead*
mittō,	mittere,	mīsī,	missum	*send*
pōnō,	pōnere,	posuī,	positum	*put, place, set up*
scrībō,	scrībere,	scripsī,	scriptum	*write*

Exercise X

A.

1. Magister puerōs dūcit.
2. Poēta verba scrībēbat.
3. Librōs et epistulās scrībimus.
4. Vir librōs pōnet.
5. Epistulās mittētis.
6. Cantābis, sed nōn vocābis.
7. Librī nōn errābunt, sed poētae.
8. Agricolae librōs pōnunt.
9. Īra dominum terruerit.
10. Magistrī verba scrībēbant.
11. Puella epistulam mittet.
12. Epistulam nōn vīdimus.
13. Deus virōs et puerōs dūcit.
14. Rēgīnae magistrum servāverant.
15. Aquam nōn mittēbātis.
16. Puellae et puerī patriam amant.
17. Deī facta, nōn verba, laudāvērunt.
18. Rēgīnae agricolās dūcunt.
19. Agrōs et silvās, sed nōn aquam, vīdistis.
20. Umbra puellam nōn vulnerābit.

B.

1. We will lead boys and girls.
2. I used to write letters, not books.
3. You (sg.) are going to write a letter.
4. The poets send books.
5. I will send the letter.
6. The master had advised the poet.
7. She frightens men, not girls.
8. The teachers will not be mistaken.
9. They wounded the queen but not the poet.
10. I am placing books.
11. God will send water.
12. The farmer has prepared the field.
13. The teacher was leading the men.
14. Girls are holding the gate.
15. Boys do not write letters, but men do.
16. We had praised the gods and the men.
17. I love woods and fields.
18. You (sg.) were writing words.
19. We will have sung the deeds.
20. You (pl.) have not feared water.

Lesson XI

THIRD CONJUGATION: CONSONANT VERBS
Perfect System Active Voice

To find the perfect stem of a third conjugation verb, remove the final -ī from the third principal part:

$$\frac{\begin{array}{r}\text{DŪXĪ}\\ \text{-ī}\end{array}}{\text{DŪX-}}$$

The perfect, pluperfect and future perfect tenses are formed by adding endings to the perfect stem.

The endings are the same as in the first and second conjugations.

PERFECT TENSE

Singular	perfect stem + ending			
1st person	dūxī	*I led,*	*- have led,*	*- did lead*
2nd person	dūxistī	*you led,*	*- have led,*	*- did lead*
3rd person	dūxit	*he/she/it led,*	*- has led,*	*- did lead*
Plural				
1st person	dūximus	*we led,*	*- have led,*	*- did lead*
2nd person	dūxistis	*you led,*	*- have led,*	*- did lead*
3rd person	dūxērunt	*they led,*	*- have led,*	*- did lead*

PLUPERFECT TENSE

Singular	perfect stem + ending	
1st person	dūxeram	*I had led*
2nd person	dūxerās	*you had led*
3rd person	dūxerat	*he/she/it had led*
Plural		
1st person	dūxerāmus	*we had led*
2nd person	dūxerātis	*you had led*
3rd person	dūxerant	*they had led*

FUTURE PERFECT TENSE

Singular	perfect stem + ending	
1st person	dūxerō	*I will have led*
2nd person	dūxeris	*you will have led*
3rd person	dūxerit	*he/she/it will have led*
Plural		
1st person	dūxerimus	*we will have led*
2nd person	dūxeritis	*you will have led*
3rd person	dūxerint	*they will have led*

RULE: When the subject consists of two or more nouns joined by **et**, the verb must be plural:

Magister et rēgīna puellam <u>laudant</u>.

22

Vocabulary XI

1ˢᵗ Declension Nouns (like **puella**)				2ⁿᵈ Declension Nouns (like **dominus**)			
dea,	deae,*	f.	*goddess*	nūntius,	nūntiī,	m.	*messenger*
fīlia,	fīliae,*	f.	*daughter*	fīlius,	fīliī,	m.	*son*

* The dative and ablative plurals are **deābus** and **filiābus**.

Exercise XI

A.

1. Fīlia et fīlius nuntium mīsērunt.
2. Poēta librōs posuerat.
3. Librōs et epistulās scrīpserāmus.
4. Librum scrīpsistī.
5. Agricola aquam dūcēbat.
6. Rēgīna et nuntius cantābant.
7. Agricola et dominus librum vīdērunt.
8. Poēta et nuntius agrum tenent.
9. Magister et dominus nuntiōs nōn mīserant.
10. Puer et magister epistulās scrīpsērunt.
11. Rēgīna et dea nuntium dūxerint.
12. Aqua et umbra agrum servāvērunt.
13. Rēgīna et fīlia epistulās mittent.
14. Fīlius aquam portāvit, sed librum nōn mīsit.
15. Deī facta, nōn verba amant.
16. Vir nuntium mīserat, sed nuntius errāvit.
17. Umbram vidēs, sed nōn videō.
18. Deī virōs terruerant et monuerant.
19. Nuntium mīsī.
20. Rēgīna puerōs et puellās vīdit.
21. Librum posuistī.
22. Silvam vidēmus, et silva poētās terret.
23. Fīlia aquam portat.
24. Epistulam, nōn librum, mīserāmus.

B.

1. The queen and the poet have sent letters.
2. You (sg.) led the men and boys.
3. A son and a daughter had placed the books.
4. You (sg.) will have written a letter.
5. We had sent a book.
6. The boy and the girl feared shadows.
7. We praised the field.
8. The girls and boys fear forests and fields.
9. The boys and girls were not afraid of the gods.
10. I have carried the books.
11. The gods will not frighten the boys and girls.
12. The queen and the daughters will praise the god.
13. The messengers and the teacher will have written letters.
14. The gods and a book will have led the native land.
15. The gods and goddesses will not hurt the queen.

Lesson XII

ADJECTIVES

ADJECTIVES are words that modify nouns.

FIRST AND SECOND DECLENSION ADJECTIVES have three sets of TERMINATIONS, or endings: one for masculine forms, one for feminine and one for neuter.

First and second declension masculine adjectives are declined like second declension masculine nouns (e.g. **dominus**). Feminine adjectives are declined like first declension nouns (e.g. **puella**). Neuter adjectives are declined like second declension neuter nouns (e.g. **verbum**).

Example: **bonus, bona, bonum** *good*

Singular	masculine	feminine	neuter
Nominative	bon**us**	bona	bon**um**
Genitive	bon**ī**	bonae	bon**ī**
Dative	bon**ō**	bonae	bon**ō**
Accusative	bon**um**	bon**am**	bon**um**
Ablative	bon**ō**	bon**ā**	bon**ō**
Plural			
Nominative	bon**ī**	bonae	bona
Genitive	bon**ōrum**	bon**ārum**	bon**ōrum**
Dative	bon**īs**	bon**īs**	bon**īs**
Accusative	bon**ōs**	bon**ās**	bona
Ablative	bon**īs**	bon**īs**	bon**īs**

RULE: An adjective agrees with the word it modifies in case, number, and gender. This is the **SECOND RULE OF CONCORD**.

Puella bona librōs amat.   Puella bonōs librōs amat.
The good girl loves books.   *The girl loves good books.*

Two or more adjectives modifying the same noun are usually joined by **et** which is not translated in English.

Puella bonōs et longōs librōs amat.
The girl loves good, long books.

One adjective modifying nouns of different genders may be repeated with each noun in Latin.

Puer bonōs librōs et bona verba amat.
The boy loves good books and good words.

Vocabulary XII

1ˢᵗ and 2ⁿᵈ Declension Adjectives (like **bonus**)							
Masculine	Feminine	Neuter		Masculine	Feminine	Neuter	
altus,	alta,	altum	*high, deep, tall*	multus,	multa,	multum	*much,* (pl.) *many*
bonus,	bona,	bonum	*good*	parvus,	parva,	parvum	*small, little*
magnus,	magna,	magnum	*great, large*	tuus,	tua,	tuum	*your, yours* (belonging to one person)
meus,	mea,	meum	*my, mine*				

Exercise XII

A.

1. Fīlia mea cantābit.
2. Rēgīna bona puellās parvās docet.
3. Virī magnī portās altās servābunt.
4. Magister librōs tuōs nōn portāvit.
5. Patriam meam poëtae bonī laudābant.
6. Nuntiī epistulās meās mīserint.
7. Librum magnum scrīpsērunt.
8. Deī facta multa laudāverant.
9. Agricola aquās altās timēbat.
10. Dea nuntium bonum dūxerat.
11. Rēgīna librōs multōs et bonōs vīdit.
12. Dominus virōs bonōs vulnerāverit.
13. Silvae magnae umbrās multās et altās tenuērunt.
14. Librōs multōs et epistulās multās scripserāmus et mīserāmus.
15. Puellae parvae et puerī magnī pugnābant.
16. Fīlius bonus et filia bona meum magistrum rogāverint.
17. Puellae multae altās silvās et umbrās timent, sed nōn deōs.
18. Librī meī magistrōs magnōs nōn laudant, sed monent.

B.

1. We will have praised the good native land.
2. The messengers had written and sent many letters.
3. The girls and boys fear your forests and my fields.
4. The good master has carried the great books.
5. Great anger held the good farmer.
6. My son and your teacher are carrying many great books.
7. The queen and the farmer will see many fields and forests.
8. My good teacher was warning many poets.
9. Your gods and goddesses will sing.
10. You (pl.) will have feared the great gods and goddesses.
11. My ghost will terrify the little boys and little girls.
12. Your queen and my master had fought.
13. Your son and daughter will fear my words.
14. You (sg.) were calling and praising the large men and small boys.

Lesson XIII

ADJECTIVES (continued)

Some adjectives of the first and second declension have a masculine which declines like the noun **liber**, **librī** and add their endings in the same way, dropping the **-e-** in the stem.

Example: **sacer**,   **sacra**,   **sacrum**   *holy*

Singular	masculine	feminine	neuter
Nominative	sacer	sacra	sacrum
Genitive	sacrī	sacrae	sacrī
Dative	sacrō	sacrae	sacrō
Accusative	sacrum	sacram	sacrum
Ablative	sacrō	sacrā	sacrō
Plural			
Nominative	sacrī	sacrae	sacra
Genitive	sacrōrum	sacrārum	sacrōrum
Dative	sacrīs	sacrīs	sacrīs
Accusative	sacrōs	sacrās	sacra
Ablative	sacrīs	sacrīs	sacrīs

Some adjectives have a masculine like **puer** and retain the **-e-** in the stem.

Example: **miser**,   **misera**,   **miserum**   *wretched*

Singular	masculine	feminine	neuter
Nominative	miser	misera	miserum
Genitive	miserī	miserae	miserī
Dative	miserō	miserae	miserō
Accusative	miserum	miseram	miserum
Ablative	miserō	miserā	miserō
Plural			
Nominative	miserī	miserae	misera
Genitive	miserōrum	miserārum	miserōrum
Dative	miserīs	miserīs	miserīs
Accusative	miserōs	miserās	misera
Ablative	miserīs	miserīs	miserīs

Vocabulary XIII

2nd Declension Adjectives ending in -er							
Stem drops the -e- (like **sacer**):				Stem keeps the -e- (like **miser**):			
noster,	nostra,	nostrum	*our*	miser,	misera,	miserum	*unhappy, wretched*
pulcher,	pulchra,	pulchrum	*beautiful*	līber,	lībera,	līberum	*free*
sacer,	sacra,	sacrum	*holy*				
vester,	vestra,	vestrum	*your, yours* (belonging to more than one person)				

Exercise XIII

A.

1. Portam vestram vīdistis.
2. Nostrōs nūntiōs mittam.
3. Virī miserī pugnant.
4. Librum sacrum nōn teneō.
5. Īram nostram nōn timēbātis.
6. Magistrōs līberōs laudāverint.
7. Silvae sacrae agricolam parvum terruērunt.
8. Dominī nostrī puellās pulchrās dūcunt.
9. Īra puerōs et puellās monēbat.
10. Poēta sacer multōs librōs scrībet.
11. Dominus miser meōs filiōs multōs vocāverat.
12. Agricolae līberī patriam līberam amant.
13. Fīlia tua epistulam parvam scrīpsit.
14. Īra vestra puellās miserās terruerat.
15. Facta sacra laudābimus.
16. Agricolae miserī agrōs parābunt.
17. Puerī multī portam magnam servābant.
18. Nuntiī meī epistulās nostrās portāvērunt.
19. Verba multa et bona cantās, sed nōn scrībis.
20. Magister puerōs verba multa et bona docuerit.

B.

1. We were singing unhappy words.
2. Wretched books teach wretched deeds.
3. My wretched son wanders and sings.
4. The beautiful girl will lead the poet.
5. The free master has praised your (sg.) deeds.
6. You are frightening the wretched poet.
7. You (sg.) will contain your anger.
8. I will carry much water.
9. We will have sent many letters.
10. You (sg.) have praised my free native land.
11. Your daughter will see our woods and fields.
12. You (pl.) are preparing your gate.
13. Great teachers used to praise good poets.
14. She saw the holy books.
15. Many gods had protected our fields and our forests.
16. Free sons and daughters will sing the great native land.
17. The little boys were asking the queen and the teachers.

Lesson XIV

FOURTH CONJUGATION : Ī-VERBS
Present System Active Voice

Verbs whose second principal part ends in **-īre** belong to the **FOURTH CONJUGATION**.

To find the present stem remove the final **-re** from the second principal part.

Example: **audiō, audīre, audīvī, audītum,** *hear*

AUDĪRE

-RE

AUDĪ-

The **-ī-** of the stem shortens before another vowel and before final **-t** or **-nt**.

PRESENT TENSE

Singular	endings		present stem + ending			
1st person	-ō	→	audiō	*I hear,*	*- am hearing,*	*- do hear*
2nd person	-s	→	audīs	*you hear,*	*- are hearing,*	*- do hear*
3rd person	-t	→	audit	*he/she/it hears,*	*- is hearing,*	*- does hear*
Plural						
1st person	-mus	→	audīmus	*we hear,*	*- are hearing,*	*- do hear*
2nd person	-tis	→	audītis	*you hear,*	*- are hearing,*	*- do hear*
3rd person	-nt	→	audiunt	*they hear,*	*- are hearing,*	*- do hear*

The 3rd person plural has the vowel **-u-** between the present stem and the personal ending.

IMPERFECT TENSE

Singular	imperfect endings		present stem + ending			
1st person	-bam	→	audiĕbam	*I was hearing,*	*- heard,*	*- used to hear*
2nd person	-bās	→	audiĕbās	*you were hearing,*	*- heard,*	*- used to hear*
3rd person	-bat	→	audiĕbat	*he/she/it was hearing,*	*- heard,*	*- used to hear*
Plural						
1st person	-bāmus	→	audiĕbāmus	*we were hearing,*	*- heard,*	*- used to hear*
2nd person	-bātis	→	audiĕbātis	*you were hearing,*	*- heard,*	*- used to hear*
3rd person	-bant	→	audiĕbant	*they were hearing,*	*- heard,*	*- used to hear*

The imperfect has the vowel **-ē-** before the ending, just as in third conjugation.

PRESENT TENSE

Singular	future endings		present stem + ending		
1st person	-am	→	audiam	*I will hear,*	*- am going to hear*
2nd person	-ēs	→	audiēs	*you will hear,*	*- are going to hear*
3rd person	-et	→	audiet	*he/she/it will hear,*	*- is going to hear*
Plural					
1st person	-ēmus	→	audiēmus	*we will hear,*	*- are going to hear*
2nd person	-ētis	→	audiētis	*you will hear,*	*- are going to hear*
3rd person	-ent	→	audient	*they will hear,*	*- are going to hear*

In the fourth conjugation the future tense is marked by vowels.

Vocabulary XIV

4th Conjugation Verbs (like **audiō**)					Conjunctions	
audiō,	audīre,	audīvī,	audītum	*hear; listen to*	quod	*because*
mūniō,	mūnīre,	mūnīvī,	mūnītum	*fortify; build*	-que*	*and*
pūniō,	pūnīre,	pūnīvī,	pūnītum	*punish*		
veniō,	venīre,	vēnī,	ventum	*come*		

*The conjunction -que is added to the end of a word and is translated before the word to which it is joined.

puerī puellaeque = puerī et puellae

Exercise XIV

A.

1. Cantātis sed nōn audīmus.
2. Puellās puerōsque vocābō et venient.
3. Puerōs et virōs bonōs nōn pūnīs.
4. Dominus puellās rogābat sed nōn audiēbant.
5. Silvae aquaque agrōs nostrōs mūniēbant.
6. Bonus magister pulchram rēgīnam docēbit.
7. Puellae puerīque tua verba audiunt, quod librum bonum scrīpsistī.
8. Agricolae miserī et magnī dominī venient, quod rēgīna epistulam mīsit.
9. Verba sacra deās nōn vulnerāverant.
10. Patriam nostram servābimus quod nūntiī monuērunt.
11. Poēta magnus librōs multōs scrīpsit et tua verba factaque laudāvit.
12. Umbram magnam timeō quod puellās miserās terruit.

B.

1. You (pl.) hear my words.
2. We were fortifying the native land.
3. Ghosts used to come.
4. I was listening to my daughter.
5. They will have punished the messenger.
6. I will punish.
7. They are fortifying the gates.
8. You (sg.) had led many messengers.
9. We have not written books.
10. Deep water did not frighten the boy and the girl.
11. The unhappy teacher was carrying the big books, but not the little (ones).
12. The great queen frightens my daughter because she punishes many girls.
13. We are coming because the master has called.
14. You (pl.) were wandering and carrying your letters.
15. I will write the letter; you (sg.) will listen to my words.

Lesson XV

FOURTH CONJUGATION: Ī-VERBS

Perfect System Active Voice

To find the perfect stem of a **FOURTH CONJUGATION** verb, remove the final **-ī** from the third principal part.

$$\frac{\text{AUDĪVĪ}}{\text{AUDĪV-}} \quad \text{-ī}$$

The perfect, pluperfect and future perfect tenses are formed by adding endings to the perfect stem.

The endings are the same as for the first, second and third conjugations.

PERFECT TENSE

Singular	perfect stem + ending			
1st person	audīvī	*I heard,*	*- have heard,*	*- did hear*
2nd person	audīvistī	*you heard,*	*- have heard,*	*- did hear*
3rd person	audīvit	*he/she/it heard,*	*- has heard,*	*- did hear*
Plural				
1st person	audīvimus	*we heard,*	*- have heard,*	*- did hear*
2nd person	audīvistis	*you heard,*	*- have heard,*	*- did hear*
3rd person	audīvērunt	*they heard,*	*- have heard,*	*- did hear*

PLUPERFECT TENSE

Singular	perfect stem + ending	
1st person	audīveram	*I had heard*
2nd person	audīverās	*you had heard*
3rd person	audīverat	*he/she/it had heard*
Plural		
1st person	audīverāmus	*we had heard*
2nd person	audīverātis	*you had heard*
3rd person	audīverant	*they had heard*

FUTURE PERFECT TENSE

Singular	perfect stem + ending	
1st person	audīverō	*I will have heard*
2nd person	audīveris	*you will have heard*
3rd person	audīverit	*he/she/it will have heard*
Plural		
1st person	audīverimus	*we will have heard*
2nd person	audīveritis	*you will have heard*
3rd person	audīverint	*they will have heard*

RULE: The **GENITIVE CASE** is used to show possession. It shows to whom a thing belongs.

     Puerī liber   *the book of the boy / the boy's book*

Vocabulary XV

2ⁿᵈ Declension Nouns (like **dominus**)				2ⁿᵈ Declension Nouns (like **verbum**)			
campus,	campī,	m.	*plain, playing field*	bellum,	bellī,	n.	*war*
mūrus,	mūrī,	m.	*wall*	tēlum,	tēlī,	n.	*weapon, javelin*
servus,	servī,	m.	*slave*				
somnus,	somnī,	m.	*sleep*				
ventus,	ventī,	m.	*wind*				

Exercise XV

A.

1. Īram ventī timuimus.
2. Servī tēla dominōrum nōn portāverant.
3. Tēla puerī parvī poētam vulnerābant.
4. Deī magnī servum nōn mīsērunt.
5. Mūrōs rēgīnae nōn servābātis.
6. Servus rēgīnae cantat, quod rēgīnam nōn timet.
7. Mūrī altī agrōs campōsque servābunt.
8. Magister puerōs puellāsque pūnīverit.
9. Bellum miserum nostrōs fīliōs docēbit.
10. Mūrī puerōs et puellās tenuerint.
11. Īrās rēgīnārum timuī, quod servōs miserōs pūnīverant.
12. Fīliī et fīliae deae bonae magnās aquās patriae amāvērunt.
13. Servī magna tēla bellī sacrī nōn portābunt.
14. Deōs agrōrum silvārumque vident.
15. Nostrī poētae epistulam nōn scrīpserant, quod errābant et cantābant.

B.

1. You sent the messenger of the teacher.
2. The gates of the wall will have guarded the teacher's little girls and little boys.
3. Your (pl.) poets will not praise the wars of the gods and goddesses.
4. The sacred books of the queen hold the letters of the poets.
5. The waters were carrying the men of our native land.
6. We have heard the beautiful queen, small girls and miserable boys.
7. Many farmers send the letters of the poets, but not of the master.
8. Your (sg.) forests terrified the small girls, because they held many shadows.
9. The native land's queen will fear my anger, but not yours.
10. The beautiful book of the poet praises the weapons of war, because they have saved the native land.
11. The wretched slaves were carrying the books of the master, because he was fighting.
12. The poets ask the miserable daughters and the son of the master.

31

Lesson XVI

THIRD CONJUGATION: I-STEM VERBS
Present System Active Voice

Some third conjugation verbs resemble fourth conjugation verbs in the present system. Such verbs can be recognized from their first principal part, which ends in **-iō**, and second principal part, which ends in **-ere**. The present stem of these verbs ends in **–i**. They are called **THIRD CONJUGATION I-STEM VERBS**.

Example: **capiō, capere, cēpī, captum,** *take*

In the imperfect and future tenses, third conjugation I-stem verbs are conjugated like **audiō**. In the present tense, they are conjugated like **audiō** in the first person singular and third person plural. Elsewhere in the present tense they are conjugated like **dūcō**, with a short **-i-** joining stem to ending, instead of the long **-ī-** seen in **audiō**.

PRESENT TENSE

Singular	endings		present stem + ending			
1st person	**-ō**	→	capi**ō**	*I take,*	*- am taking,*	*- do take*
2nd person	**-s**	→	capi**s**	*you take,*	*- are taking,*	*- do take*
3rd person	**-t**	→	capi**t**	*he/she/it takes,*	*- is taking,*	*- does take*
Plural						
1st person	**-mus**	→	capi**mus**	*we take,*	*- are taking,*	*- do take*
2nd person	**-tis**	→	capi**tis**	*you take,*	*- are taking,*	*- do take*
3rd person	**-nt**	→	capiu**nt**	*they take,*	*- are taking,*	*- do take*

IMPERFECT TENSE

Singular	imperfect endings		present stem + ending			
1st person	**-bam**	→	capiē**bam**	*I was taking,*	*- took,*	*- used to take*
2nd person	**-bās**	→	capiē**bās**	*you were taking,*	*- took,*	*- used to take*
3rd person	**-bat**	→	capiē**bat**	*he/she/it was taking,*	*- took,*	*- used to take*
Plural						
1st person	**-bāmus**	→	capiē**bāmus**	*we were taking,*	*- took,*	*- used to take*
2nd person	**-bātis**	→	capiē**bātis**	*you were taking,*	*- took,*	*- used to take*
3rd person	**-bant**	→	capiē**bant**	*they were taking,*	*- took,*	*- used to take*

The imperfect has the vowel **-ē-** before the ending, as in the fourth conjugation.

FUTURE TENSE

Singular	future endings		present stem + ending		
1st person	**-am**	→	capi**am**	*I will take,*	*- am going to take*
2nd person	**-ēs**	→	capi**ēs**	*you will take,*	*- are going to take*
3rd person	**-et**	→	capi**et**	*he/she/it will take,*	*- is going to take*
Plural					
1st person	**-ēmus**	→	capi**ēmus**	*we will take,*	*- are going to take*
2nd person	**-ētis**	→	capi**ētis**	*you will take,*	*- are going to take*
3rd person	**-ent**	→	capi**ent**	*they will take,*	*- are going to take*

In the third conjugation the future tense is marked by vowels.

32

Vocabulary XVI

3rd Conjugation I-Stem Verbs (like **capiō**)					1st Declension Nouns (like **puella**)			
capiō,	capere,	cēpī,	captum	*take, seize, capture*	ōra,	ōrae,	f.	*shore, rim, edge*
faciō,	facere,	fēcī,	factum	*make, so*	terra,	terrae,	f.	*land, earth, a country*
fugiō,	fugere,	fūgī,	fugitūrus	*flee, run away, avoid*				

Exercise XVI

A.

1. Tēla servōrum capiēbāmus.
2. Ōram terrae fugiēmus.
3. Servī filiōs dominōrum fugiunt.
4. Librum tuum nōn capiam.
5. Verba bona scrībitis et facta magna faciētis.
6. Mūrum altum posuimus.
7. Campum sacrum mūniēbant.
8. Virī līberī librōs bonōs scrībunt.
9. Īram et tēla deōrum fugiēmus.
10. Miserōs puerōs virōsque sacrōs fugitis.
11. Servus miser agrōs dominī fugiēbat, quod tēla dominī servum vulnerāverant.
12. Agricola bonus servum miserum servāvit.
13. Dominus nuntium mīsit, quod servus miser fūgerat.
14. Nuntius servum dominī capiet.
15. Sed somnus dominum fugiet, quod servum miserum bonumque pūnīvit.

B.

1. You (pl.) will capture the queen's fields.
2. We were avoiding the teacher's wrath.
3. We saw your (sg.) book and took (it).
4. The gods make the good books of holy poets.
5. I was taking the weapon of the master.
6. We have asked the beautiful goddess, but you have fortified our shore.
7. The anger of the gods frightens the small farmer.
8. We will capture your (sg.) sons and daughters, because you are making a high wall.
9. You (sg.) were making the wall because we were capturing your sons and daughters.
10. Wretched war will punish the men of your (pl.) native land.
11. The anger of the gods will frighten the queen of the land.
12. Poets write books, but men do great deeds.

Lesson XVII

THIRD CONJUGATION: I-STEM VERBS
Perfect System Active Voice

To find the perfect stem of any verb, remove the final **-ī** from the third principal part:

$$\begin{array}{r} \text{CĒPĪ} \\ \underline{\text{-Ī}} \\ \text{CĒP-} \end{array}$$

The perfect, pluperfect, and future perfect tenses are formed by adding endings to the perfect stem. The endings of the perfect system are the same for all verbs.

PERFECT TENSE

Singular	perfect stem + ending			
1ˢᵗ person	cēp**ī**	*I took,*	*- have taken,*	*- did take*
2ⁿᵈ person	cēp**istī**	*you took,*	*- have taken,*	*- did take*
3ʳᵈ person	cēp**it**	*he/she/it took,*	*- has taken,*	*- did take*
Plural				
1ˢᵗ person	cēp**imus**	*we took,*	*- have taken,*	*- did take*
2ⁿᵈ person	cēp**istis**	*you took,*	*- have taken,*	*- did take*
3ʳᵈ person	cēp**ērunt**	*they took,*	*- have taken,*	*- did take*

PLUPERFECT TENSE

Singular	perfect stem + ending	
1ˢᵗ person	cēp**eram**	*I had taken*
2ⁿᵈ person	cēp**erās**	*you had taken*
3ʳᵈ person	cēp**erat**	*he/she/it had taken*
Plural		
1ˢᵗ person	cēp**erāmus**	*we had taken*
2ⁿᵈ person	cēp**erātis**	*you had taken*
3ʳᵈ person	cēp**erant**	*they had taken*

FUTURE PERFECT TENSE

Singular	perfect stem + ending	
1ˢᵗ person	cēp**erō**	*I will have taken*
2ⁿᵈ person	cēp**eris**	*you will have taken*
3ʳᵈ person	cēp**erit**	*he/she/it will have taken*
Plural		
1ˢᵗ person	cēp**erimus**	*we will have taken*
2ⁿᵈ person	cēp**eritis**	*you will have taken*
3ʳᵈ person	cēp**erint**	*they will have taken*

Prepositions

Latin **PREPOSITIONS** govern objects in the accusative or ablative case. Learn the case governed with each preposition. The prepositions **in** (into) and **ad** (toward) govern the accusative case and show motion toward an object.

Examples:	Puellae in silvam vēnērunt.	*The girls came into the forest.*
	Ad mūrum fugit.	*He is fleeing toward the wall.*

Vocabulary XVII

3rd Conjugation I-Stem Verbs (like **capiō**)					Prepositions with Accusative	
accipiō,	accipere,	accēpī,	acceptum	*receive*	ad	*to, towards, at*
interficiō,	interficere,	interfēcī,	interfectum	*kill*	in	*into, onto, against*
1st and 2nd Declension Adjectives (like **sacer**)						
aeger,	aegra,	aegrum	*sick*			
āter,	ātra,	ātrum	*dark, black*			

Exercise XVII

A.

1. Servus miser agricolam interfēcit.
2. Ad ōram fugiēmus et pugnābimus.
3. Dominus nūntium in campum mīserat.
4. In altam aquam vēnistis.
5. Dea magna verba vestra audiet.
6. Facta bellī nōn laudābimus.
7. Bellum fūgistī et ad portam nostram vēnistī.
8. Silva ātra agricolās accipiet et terrēbit.
9. Rēgīna filiōs tuōs nōn terruit quod īram tenuit.
10. Aegrī virī deōs rogant.
11. Mea filia aegra epistulam tuam accipit.
12. In silvās ātrī deī errābātis.
13. Deī pulchrās terrās fēcerant.
14. Mūrus altus campum servābit.
15. Magister puerōs multōs nōn pūnīverit.
16. Servōs aegrōs accēpimus, sed nōn interficiēmus.
17. Deae aquam in agrōs agricolārum mittēbant.
18. Nūntiōs nostrōs in ātram umbram silvae mittēmus.
19. Dominus portās magnās multāsque in mūrum posuerat.
20. Fīliī rēgīnae ventum audīvērunt sed nōn vīdērunt.

B.

1. We will seize the great gate.
2. The waters kill the sailors.
3. The queen's slaves will receive a messenger.
4. You (pl.) were receiving books.
5. I had not listened to (=heard) my master.
6. He is fortifying a beautiful gate.
7. I have sent your (sg.) letter, but not your books.
8. The girl was not fleeing the ghost.
9. You (sg.) will carry water to the field.
10. She seized the sick boy of the free slave.
11. You (pl.) wrote the words of holy poets.
12. Weapons had killed the unhappy men.
13. The great ghost seized the slave and carried (him) into the dark forest.
14. The sick man's slaves had done many great deeds.
15. The anger of the wretched queen will frighten the little girls.
16. The homeland is calling good men and they will fight.
17. I will lead men onto the high wall, but not into deep water.
18. Teachers carry books to the shore.

Lesson XVIII

IRREGULAR VERB: SUM

The verb **sum** has irregular principal parts. In the present system, its conjugation is irregular. In the perfect system, the formation is regular from the third principal part, **fuī**. All forms must be memorized.

I	II	III	IV	
SUM,	ESSE,	FUĪ,	FUTŪRUS	*be*

PRESENT SYSTEM
PRESENT TENSE

Singular		
1st person	**sum**	*I am*
2nd person	**es**	*you are*
3rd person	**est**	*he/she/it is*

Plural		
1st person	**sumus**	*we are*
2nd person	**estis**	*you are*
3rd person	**sunt**	*they are*

IMPERFECT TENSE

Singular		
1st person	**eram**	*I was, -used to be*
2nd person	**erās**	*you were, -used to be*
3rd person	**erat**	*he/she/it was, -used to be*

Plural		
1st person	**erāmus**	*we were, -used to be*
2nd person	**erātis**	*you were, -used to be*
3rd person	**erant**	*they were, -used to be*

FUTURE TENSE

Singular		
1st person	**erō**	*I will be*
2nd person	**eris**	*you will be*
3rd person	**erit**	*he/she/it will be*

Plural		
1st person	**erimus**	*we will be*
2nd person	**eritis**	*you will be*
3rd person	**erunt**	*they will be*

PERFECT SYSTEM
PERFECT TENSE

Singular	perfect stem + ending	
1st person	**fuī**	*I have been, -was*
2nd person	**fuistī**	*you have been, -were*
3rd person	**fuit**	*he/she/it has been, -was*

Plural		
1st person	**fuimus**	*we have been, -were*
2nd person	**fuistis**	*you have been, -were*
3rd person	**fuērunt**	*they have been, -were*

IMPERFECT TENSE

Singular	perfect stem + ending	
1st person	**fueram**	*I had been*
2nd person	**fuerās**	*you had been*
3rd person	**fuerat**	*he/she/it had been*

Plural		
1st person	**fuerāmus**	*we had been*
2nd person	**fuerātis**	*you had been*
3rd person	**fuerant**	*they had been*

FUTURE TENSE

Singular	perfect stem + ending	
1st person	**fuerō**	*I will have been*
2nd person	**fueris**	*you will have been*
3rd person	**fuerit**	*he/she/it will have been*

Plural		
1st person	**fuerimus**	*we will have been*
2nd person	**fueritis**	*you will have been*
3rd person	**fuerint**	*they will have been*

The verb sum is usually a linking verb, which joins the subject to another word, either noun or adjective. That word is a **COMPLEMENT**. A noun complement is called a **PREDICATE NOUN**. An adjective complement is called a **PREDICATE ADJECTIVE**.

RULE: A predicate noun agrees with the subject of the verb in case; a predicate adjective agrees in case, number and gender.

Puella est bona.	*The girl is good.*
Agricola est bonus.	*The farmer is good.*
Vir est agricola.	*The man is a farmer.*

36

Vocabulary XVIII

Irregular Verb				1st and 2nd Declension Adjectives (like **bonus**)			
sum,	esse,	fuī,	futūrus *be*	amīcus,	amīca,	amīcum	*friendly*
2nd Declension Noun (like **dominus**)				fessus,	fessa,	fessum	*tired, exhausted*
amīcus, amīcī, m.			*friend*	īrātus,	īrāta,	īrātum	*angry*
				malus,	mala,	malum	*evil, bad, wicked*
				pius,	pia,	pium	*dutiful, devoted, loyal*

Exercise XVIII

A.

1. Rēgīna est amīca.
2. Servī erunt fessī, et ad silvam venient.
3. Pius sum; deōs amō.
4. Noster magister fuerit īrātus.
5. Erimus agricolae bonī.
6. Estis puellae malae.
7. Deī nōn fuimus.
8. Misera eris quod es fessa.
9. Aquae fuērunt pulchrae.
10. Parvī fīliī fuerant malī.
11. Mūrus erat āter et altus.
12. Puella aegra erit fessa.
13. Terra deōrum fuit sacra.
14. Magister nōn est umbra.
15. Fessus sum, et bonus erit somnus.
16. Līberae fueritis quod virī bellum pugnāvērunt.
17. Dominus īrātus malōs virōs interfēcit, quod tēla in agricolās parāverant.
18. Fīliae agricolae aquās ātrās sacrāsque amāverint.
19. Rēgīna eram, quod multās terrās tenēbam.
20. Umbra silvae ātrae fīliōs fīliāsque poētārum terrēbit.

B.

1. The gates are tall.
2. I am an angry queen.
3. The little boys have been tired.
4. The native lands will be sacred.
5. We will not be evil masters.
6. Your (pl.) sleep was good.
7. We had not been farmers, but teachers.
8. You (sg.) will be a beautiful goddess.
9. Our book was beautiful, but small.
10. The words of the poets have been friendly.
11. You (pl.) have been sick and tired.
12. My letters used to be large but are small.
13. The waters of the land terrify the miserable boys and girls.
14. We have not warned the tired boys at the gate.
15. The sick poet was carrying the letter into the native land.
16. I was hearing the sacred words of the gods and goddesses.

Lesson XIX

THIRD DECLENSION NOUNS
Masculine and Feminine

Nouns whose genitive singular ends in **-is** belong to the **THIRD DECLENSION**.

To find the stem of any Latin noun, remove the ending from the genitive singular form.

MĪLITIS	LĒGIS
-IS	-IS
MĪLIT-	LĒG-

The nominative endings for the third declension vary.

Third declension nouns are declined by adding the case endings to the noun stem.

Singular	ending		noun stem + ending	
Nominative	—	→	mīles	*soldier*
Genitive	-is	→	mīlitis	*of the soldier, soldier's*
Dative	-ī	→	mīlitī	*to / for the soldier*
Accusative	-em	→	mīlitem	*the soldier*
Ablative	-e	→	mīlite	*by / with / from the soldier*
Plural				
Nominative	-ēs	→	mīlitēs	*soldiers*
Genitive	-um	→	mīlitum	*of the soldiers, soldiers'*
Dative	-ibus	→	mīlitibus	*to / for the soldiers*
Accusative	-ēs	→	mīlitēs	*soldiers*
Ablative	-ibus	→	mīlitibus	*by / with / from the soldiers*

Third declension feminine nouns use the same endings as the masculine.

Singular	ending		noun stem + ending	
Nominative	—	→	lēx	*law*
Genitive	-is	→	lēgis	*of the law, law's*
Dative	-ī	→	lēgī	*to / for the law*
Accusative	-em	→	lēgem	*the law*
Ablative	-e	→	lēge	*by / with / from the law*
Plural				
Nominative	-ēs	→	lēgēs	*laws*
Genitive	-um	→	lēgum	*of the laws, laws'*
Dative	-ibus	→	lēgibus	*to / for the laws*
Accusative	-ēs	→	lēgēs	*laws*
Ablative	-ibus	→	lēgibus	*by / with / from the laws*

Vocabulary XIX

1st Declension Nouns (like **puella**)			
dux,	ducis,	m.	*leader*
lex,	lēgis,	f.	*law*
mīles,	mīlitis,	m.	*soldier*
soror,	sorōris,	f.	*sister*
vox	vōcis,	f.	*voice*

Exercise XIX

A.

1. Magnus dominus sorōrēs aegrās vocābit.
2. Vestrae vōcēs sunt miserae.
3. Mīlitēs epistulās accipient.
4. Rēgīna ducem mīlitum nōn rogat.
5. Vōcem piae rēgīnae audīveram.
6. Mīlitēs bellum fugiunt, et dux mīlitēs pūniet.
7. Dux mīlitum īrātās puellās ad terram portāverit.
8. Dux lēgem nōn fēcit, sed patriam amāvit.
9. Mea soror fuerit magna rēgīna.
10. Rēgīna patriae errābat et cantābat.
11. Sacra dea agricolās amīcōs et magistrōs pūnīvit.
12. Īra magistrī puellās et puerōs monuit.
13. Tua filia pulchrōs librōs fēcerat, sed nōn laudāverat.
14. Fessus nuntius epistulās pulchrās in librum pōnēbat.
15. Sorōrēs filiāsque capiēbāmus, et filiās piās in campum dūcēbāmus.
16. Nostrī mīlitēs sacrōs poētās nōn audiēbant.
17. Īrāta dea malōs puerōs interfēcit, quod pugnāverant.
18. Dominus lēgēs bellī scrībēbat et librōs magnōs parābat.

B.

1. The sick soldier was guarding the gates of the native land.
2. The laws of the dutiful master punish the bad boys and girls.
3. The ghost of your (sg.) sister wanders into the lands.
4. The loyal slave has received the sister of the farmer.
5. The sister of the master loved the books and letters of the poets.
6. We will have fled the anger of the leader and the shadows of the forest.
7. The good messenger will send the sons and daughters to the plain.
8. The evil queen received the teachers, poets, and soldiers into the native land.
9. You (pl.) have heard the beautiful voices of the holy goddesses.
10. The leaders of the slaves will have killed the tired messengers of the master.
11. The friendly wind was carrying my words toward the shore.
12. Our wretched teacher had taught the beautiful words of the poet.

Lesson XX

THIRD DECLENSION NOUNS
Neuter

Neuter nouns of the third declension obey the neuter law: The nominative and accusative forms are the same, and the plurals of those cases ends in **-a**.

To find the stem of any Latin noun, remove the ending from the genitive singular.

Example: **opus**, **operis**, n.

OPERIS
_____-IS
OPER-

Singular	ending		noun stem + ending	
Nominative	—	→	opus	*work*
Genitive	**-is**	→	oper**is**	*of the work*
Dative	**-ī**	→	oper**ī**	*to / for work*
Accusative	—	→	opus	*the work*
Ablative	**-e**	→	oper**e**	*by / with / from the work*
Plural				
Nominative	**-a**	→	oper**a**	*works*
Genitive	**-um**	→	oper**um**	*of the works*
Dative	**-ibus**	→	oper**ibus**	*to / for the works*
Accusative	**-a**	→	oper**a**	*works*
Ablative	**-ibus**	→	oper**ibus**	*by / with / from the works*

Example: **carmen**, **carminis**, n.

CARMINIS
_____-IS
CARMIN-

Singular	ending		noun stem + ending	
Nominative	—	→	carmen	*song*
Genitive	**-is**	→	carmin**is**	*of a song*
Dative	**-ī**	→	carmin**ī**	*to / for a song*
Accusative	—	→	carmen	*song*
Ablative	**-e**	→	carmin**e**	*by / with / from a song*
Plural				
Nominative	**-a**	→	carmin**a**	*songs*
Genitive	**-um**	→	carmin**um**	*of songs*
Dative	**-ibus**	→	carmin**ibus**	*to / for songs*
Accusative	**-a**	→	carmin**a**	*songs*
Ablative	**-ibus**	→	carmin**ibus**	*by / with / from songs*

Vocabulary XX

3rd Declension Nouns (like **carmen** and **opus**)				1st and 2nd Declension Adjective (like **bonus**)			
carmen,	carminis,	n.	*song*	longus,	longa,	longum	*long*
lītus,	lītoris,	n.	*shore, coast, beach*				
flūmen,	flūminis,	n.	*river*				
nōmen,	nōminis,	n.	*name*				
onus,	oneris,	n.	*burden*				
opus,	operis,	n.	*work, task*				

Exercise XX

A.

1. Puellae pulchrae carmen longum cantābant.
2. Flūmen longum mīlitēs fessōs terrēbit.
3. Ducis servī onus magnum ad lītus portābunt.
4. Opera factaque virōrum piōrum amābimus.
5. Lītus terrae erat longum, sed puer nōn timēbat.
6. Nōmina mīlitum piōrum scrībam.
7. Rēgīna lēgēs malās facit quod est īrāta.
8. Fessus mīles vōcem amīcae puellae audīvit et fūgit.
9. Onera servōrum ad flūmen portāverās.
10. Malus magister fessōs puerōs multa verba docuerat.
11. Mea soror bona puerum parvum ad flūmen dūxit.
12. Vōcēs puellārum pulchrārum erant amīcae.

B.

1. The long river carries water to the shore.
2. The good slaves sang many beautiful songs.
3. Tired soldiers were carrying burdens of the leaders.
4. The gods will praise the works of loyal men.
5. We have heard the voice of your (sg.) sister.
6. I fear sleep and the song of the evil master.
7. The friendly teacher will have done the task of (his) slaves.
8. The slaves were wretched because they were carrying great burdens.
9. Your (pl.) leader has called my sons to the war.
10. You (pl.) saw the dark shadows and fled into the woods.
11. You (sg.) have carried my name and my words to your homeland.
12. Into my book I will place the words and deeds of a great man.

Lesson XXI

THIRD DECLENSION NOUNS

I-Stems

Some third declension nouns have a characteristic **-i-** in the genitive plural of all genders. Some neuter nouns have **-i-** in the ablative singular and nominative, genitive, and accusative plural. These words are called **I-STEMS**.

To find the stem of any Latin noun remove the genitive singular ending.

NĀVIS	URBIS	MARIS
-IS	-IS	-IS
NĀV-	URB-	MAR-

I-Stems fit into three categories:

PARISYLLABICS

PARISYLLABIC words, whose nominative and genitive singular forms have an equal number of syllables (e.g. **nāvis, nāvis** f. *ship*).

	Singular	Plural	
Nominative	nāv**is**	nāv**ēs**	
Genitive	nāv**is**	nāv**ium**	←
Dative	nāv**ī**	nāv**ibus**	
Accusative	nāv**em**	nāv**īs** (-**ēs**)	
Ablative	nāv**e**	nāv**ibus**	

MONOSYLLABICS WITH STEM ENDING IN 2 CONSONANTS

MONOSYLLABIC words, whose stem ends in two consonants (e.g. **urbs, urbis**, f. *city*).

	Singular	Plural	
Nominative	urb**s**	urb**ēs**	
Genitive	urb**is**	urb**ium**	←
Dative	urb**ī**	urb**ibus**	
Accusative	urb**em**	urb**īs** (-**ēs**)	
Ablative	urb**e**	urb**ibus**	

NEUTERS ENDING IN −E, -AL, -AR

Neuter nouns, whose nominative ends in **-e**, **-al**, **-ar** (e.g. **mare, maris**, n. *sea*).

	Singular		Plural	
Nominative	mar**e**		mar**ia**	←
Genitive	mar**is**		mar**ium**	←
Dative	mar**ī**		mar**ibus**	
Accusative	mar**e**		mar**ia**	←
Ablative	mar**ī**	←	mar**ibus**	

Vocabulary XXI

3rd Declension I-Stem Nouns (like **nāvis**, **urbs**, and **mare**)			
cīvis,	cīvis,	m. or f.	*citizen*
gēns,	gentis,	f.	*tribe, nation*
mare,	maris,	n.	*sea*
nāvis,	nāvis,	f.	*ship*
urbs,	urbis,	f.	*city*

Exercise XXI

A.

1. Īrātus cīvis rēgīnam interfēcit.
2. Sorōrēs vōcem maris ventīque audiunt.
3. Nōmen urbis est Rōma.
4. Nāvis parva aquam portāvit.
5. Nōmina mīlitum et cīvium nōn vocābātis.
6. Fīlia agricolae epistulam longam accipiēbat.
7. Flūmina ad ōrās marium ātrōrum errābunt.
8. Cīvēs urbem fūgērunt, quod multās nāvīs vīderant.
9. Opera poētārum, sed nōn urbīs gentium servāverimus.
10. Agricolae onera magna tenēbunt, sed nōn portābunt.
11. Dux mīlitum nūntiōs piōs ad lītus maris mīserat.
12. Librī carminaque poētārum multa verba pulchra tenuerint.
13. Fīliī cīvium fessī erant, sed fīliae miserae erant.
14. Īrātae gentēs aquam ad agrōs cīvium nōn portāvērunt quod aegrae sunt.
15. Verba sorōris meum servum vulnerant, sed carmina poētārum nōn vulnerant.
16. Vōcem deī et parvī puerī īram nōn timuistī.

B.

1. The song of the citizens is long.
2. The tribes will guard the gates of the city, but not the black ships.
3. We wrote the names of the ships.
4. The letters of the tribes warned the citizens.
5. The laws of the city punished the evil farmers and masters.
6. The shades of the forests had terrified the queen of the tribe.
7. The black ships of the native land carried the books of the poets to a friendly country.
8. I am a loyal citizen, but not a good farmer.
9. The winds of the sea punished the sick little girl and the master of the ship.
10. You (sg.) were praising the holy laws of your native land.
11. The friendly queen will advise the master of the slaves.
12. Our soldiers had wandered into the fields of the angry leader.
13. We fled to the shore of the sea, but the winds were great.
14. The wretched goddess and great god fight because they are angry.
15. The good messengers will carry my angry words to the man.

Lesson XXII

FIRST CONJUGATION: Ā-VERBS
Present System Passive Voice

The **ACTIVE VOICE** expresses what the subject does; the **PASSIVE VOICE** expresses what is done to the subject.

Examples: The boy calls. (active)

The boy is called. (passive)

PRESENT TENSE

Singular	endings		present stem + ending		
1ˢᵗ person	**-or**	→	am**or**	*I am (being) loved*	
2ⁿᵈ person	**-ris**	→	amā**ris**	*you are (being) loved*	
3ʳᵈ person	**-tur**	→	amā**tur**	*he/she/it is (being) loved*	
Plural					
1ˢᵗ person	**-mur**	→	amā**mur**	*we are (being) loved*	
2ⁿᵈ person	**-minī**	→	amā**minī**	*you are (being) loved*	
3ʳᵈ person	**-ntur**	→	amā**ntur**	*they are (being) loved*	

IMPERFECT TENSE

Singular	endings		present stem + ending		
1ˢᵗ person	**-bar**	→	amā**bar**	*I was being loved*	*-used to be loved*
2ⁿᵈ person	**-bāris**	→	amā**bāris**	*you were being loved*	*-used to be loved*
3ʳᵈ person	**-bātur**	→	amā**bātur**	*he/she/it was being loved*	*-used to be loved*
Plural					
1ˢᵗ person	**-bāmur**	→	amā**bāmur**	*we were being loved*	*-used to be loved*
2ⁿᵈ person	**-bāminī**	→	amā**bāminī**	*you were being loved*	*-used to be loved*
3ʳᵈ person	**-bāntur**	→	amā**bantur**	*they were being loved*	*-used to be loved*

FUTURE TENSE

Singular	endings		present stem + ending		
1ˢᵗ person	**-bor**	→	amā**bor**	*I will be loved*	
2ⁿᵈ person	**-beris**	→	amā**beris**	*you will be loved*	
3ʳᵈ person	**-bitur**	→	amā**bitur**	*he/she/it will be loved*	
Plural					
1ˢᵗ person	**-bimur**	→	amā**bimur**	*we will be loved*	
2ⁿᵈ person	**-biminī**	→	amā**biminī**	*you will be loved*	
3ʳᵈ person	**-buntur**	→	amā**buntur**	*they will be loved*	

- A passive verb cannot have a direct object.

The person by whom something is done is expressed by the ablative case with the preposition **ab/ā** (*by*). This is called the **ABLATIVE OF PERSONAL AGENT**.

Example: Tēla ab <u>mīlitibus</u> portantur.   *Weapons are being carried <u>by soldiers</u>.*

The means by which something is done is expressed by the ablative without a preposition. This is called the **ABLATIVE OF MEANS**.

Example: Mīlitēs <u>tēlīs</u> vulnerantur.   *The soldiers are being wounded <u>by weapons</u>.*

44

Vocabulary XXII

1st Conjugation Verbs (like **amō**)				
monstrō,	monstrāre,	monstrāvi,	monstrātum	*show*
nuntiō,	nuntiāre,	nuntiāvī,	nuntiātum	*report, announce*

1st Declension Masculine Nouns (like **poēta**)				Prepositions with Accusative
incola,	incolae,	m.	*inhabitant*	ab/ā* + abl. *by*
nauta,	nautae,	m.	*sailor*	* (The shortened form may be used before a consonant.)
pīrāta,	pīrātae,	m.	*pirate*	
scrība,	scrībae,	m.	*writer, secretary*	

Exercise XXII

A.

1. Rogābitur.
2. Mōnstrantur.
3. Portāberis.
4. Carmen ā nautīs cantātur.
5. Ā puellā vocāminī.
6. Vulnerābimur ā scrībā malō.
7. Tēlīs vulnerābāminī.
8. Īrā deōrum servābimur.
9. Verbīs incolārum īrātōrum laudābāminī.
10. Puellae verbīs poētārum servābuntur.
11. Nautae īrātī pīrātās nōn laudābunt.
12. Nōmina incolārum terrae nūntiābantur.
13. Epistula meae fīliae ā sorōre tuā monstrābitur.
14. Nautae fessī ā pīrātā vulnerābuntur.
15. Ā virīs tēla nōn parābantur, quod bellum nōn nūntiābātur.
16. Carmina multa cantābantur et rēgīna laudābātur.
17. Onera magna et aqua ā servīs ad dominōs portantur.
18. Vōcēs mīlitum incolās miserōs silvae terruērunt.
19. Cīvēs servīque ad urbem vēnērunt et portam mūniunt.
20. Eris nauta līber quod nāvem meam servāvistī.

B.

1. We are being called.
2. I was being carried.
3. The boy is wounded by your (sg.) words.
4. You (sg.) will be shown.
5. The songs were being sung by poets.
6. You (pl.) are not being praised by your teachers.
7. Good poets write beautiful songs.
8. The great queen's laws were being announced.
9. The good secretary will be praised.
10. Your name is being announced.
11. You (pl.) were being asked.
12. She was being loved by (her) friends.
13. Burdens are carried by the inhabitants.
14. I am coming to the shore of my native land.
15. The high walls of our city will be guarded.
16. I will receive the teachers' books and letters.
17. The poets' songs are being sung by the friendly citizens.
18. The pirates' leaders were leading the soldiers onto the black ships.

Lesson XXIII

FIRST CONJUGATION: Ā-VERBS
Perfect System Passive Voice

Passive forms of the perfect system consist of two words: the Fourth Principal Part (called the **PERFECT PASSIVE PARTICIPLE**) declined like **bonus** and a form of **sum**.

PERFECT TENSE

Singular	ending + form of sum				
1st person	-us / -a sum	→	amātus / -a sum	*I was loved,*	*-have been loved*
2nd person	-us / -a es	→	amātus / -a es	*you were loved,*	*-have been loved*
3rd person	-us / -a / -um est	→	amātus / -a / -um est	*he/she/it was loved,*	*-has been loved*
Plural					
1st person	-ī / -ae sumus	→	amātī / -ae sumus	*we were loved,*	*-have been loved*
2nd person	-ī / -ae estis	→	amātī / -ae estis	*you were loved,*	*-have been loved*
3rd person	-ī / -ae / -a sunt	→	amātī / -ae / -a sunt	*they were loved,*	*-have been loved*

PLUPERFECT TENSE

Singular	ending + form of sum			
1st person	-us / -a eram	→	amātus / -a eram	*I had been loved*
2nd person	-us / -a erās	→	amātus / -a erās	*you had been loved*
3rd person	-us / -a / -um erat	→	amātus / -a / -um erat	*he/she/it had been loved*
Plural				
1st person	-ī / -ae erāmus	→	amātī / -ae erāmus	*we had been loved*
2nd person	-ī / -ae erātis	→	amātī / -ae erātis	*you had been loved*
3rd person	-ī / -ae / -a erant	→	amātī / -ae / -a erant	*they had been loved*

FUTURE PERFECT TENSE

Singular	ending + form of sum			
1st person	-us / -a erō	→	amātus / -a erō	*I will have been loved*
2nd person	-us / -a eris	→	amātus / -a eris	*you will have been loved*
3rd person	-us / -a / -um erit	→	amātus / -a / -um erit	*he/she/it will have been loved*
Plural				
1st person	-ī / -ae erimus	→	amātī / -ae erimus	*we will have been loved*
2nd person	-ī / -ae eritis	→	amātī / -ae eritis	*you will have been loved*
3rd person	-ī / -ae / -a erunt	→	amātī / -ae / -a erunt	*they will have been loved*

In the passive of the perfect system, the perfect passive participle agrees with the subject in case, number, and gender.

Singular		**Plural**	
Puer amātus est.	*The boy was loved.*	Puerī amātī sunt.	*The boys were loved.*
Puella amāta est.	*The girl was loved.*	Puellae amātae sunt.	*The girls were loved.*
Nōmen amātum est.	*The name was loved.*	Nōmina amāta sunt.	*The names were loved.*

When an adjective modifies two or more nouns of different genders, the adjective agrees with the masculine rather than with the feminine. This also applies to the perfect passive participle in the perfect passive system.

Puer et puella laudātī sunt.   *The boy and the girl were praised.*

46

Vocabulary XXIII

3rd Declension Neuter Nouns (like **carmen** and **opus**)			
caput,	capitis,	n.	*head*
corpus,	corporis,	n.	*body*
iter,	itineris,	n.	*journey, road, way* (iter facere = *make a journey, march*)
iūs,	iūris,	n.	*a right, law*
pectus,	pectoris,	n.	*breast, chest, heart*

Exercise XXIII

A.

1. Iter mōnstrātum est.
2. Vocātī erātis.
3. Nāvēs mōnstrātae sunt.
4. Corpus vulnerātum erit.
5. Porta servāta erat.
6. Carmen erit longum.
7. Mea soror laudāta est, quod vōx est pulchra.
8. Ā puellā rogātae sumus.
9. Iūra patriae nūntiāta erunt.
10. In silvam ātram errābās.
11. Tuum pectus tēlō vulneratum est.
12. Gēns mala et cīvēs nōn pūnītī erant.
13. Multae nāvēs pīrātārum ā nautīs nostrīs captae sunt.
14. Corpus ducis pīrātārum ā mīlitibus monstrābitur.
15. Caput pīrātae malī ad lītus portātum est.
16. Corpus meum est fessum, sed pectus pium.
17. Mīlitēs in silvās iter fēcērunt et ad campum vēnērunt.
18. Fīliī fīliaeque agricolārum ad agrōs nōn vocātī sunt.

B.

1. The soldier's breast has been wounded.
2. Many songs of poets will be sung.
3. The inhabitants will make many journeys.
4. Burdens had been carried.
5. Sick sons are loved by (their) sister.
6. Water was carried to the master.
7. The rights of free men will be praised.
8. The inhabitants are angry.
9. We did not see the head of your ghost.
10. Our slaves will be sick and tired.
11. The letters have been prepared.
12. The country's name will have been praised.
13. We have been preserved by the rights of nations.
14. We guarded our heads, but our bodies were wounded.
15. The queen warned the citizens of the city, but she was mistaken.
16. The gods will send wind to the sea and will punish the sailors.
17. The leader of free men will be a good teacher.
18. The hearts of the loyal soldiers were captured by the girls of the free nation.

Lesson XXIV

PREPOSITIONS

These prepositions are followed by an object in the ablative case:

PREPOSITIONS THAT ARE FOLLOWED BY THE ABLATIVE	
ā/ab	*from; away from; by*
cum	*with, along with*
dē	*about, concerning; down from*
ē/ex	*from, out of*
in	*in, on*
prō	*in front of; on behalf of*
sine	*without*
sub	*under*

Most other prepositions in Latin are followed by the accusative case.
- **Ab** and **ex** may drop the final consonant before a word beginning with a consonant other than **h**.
- A few prepositions, like **in**, are followed by both the accusative and ablative cases. The meaning of these prepositions depends on the case of their object.

in urbem	<u>*into*</u> *the city*
in urbe	<u>*in*</u> *the city*

ABLATIVE CONSTRUCTIONS WHICH USE THESE PREPOSITIONS

ABLATIVE OF PERSONAL AGENT – The personal agent with a passive verb is expressed by the ablative with the preposition ā/ab.

Puella <u>ā rēgīnā</u> amāta est.   *The girl was loved <u>by the queen</u>.*

ABLATIVE OF ACCOMPANIMENT – Accompaniment or association is often expressed by **cum** followed by the ablative. *With* when it means *together with* or *in company with* is translated by **cum** followed by the ablative.

Puella <u>cum sorōre</u> cantat.   *The girl sings <u>with the sister</u>.*

ABLATIVE OF PLACE WHERE – Place *where* or *in which* is expressed by the ablative with the preposition **in**.

<u>In urbe</u> manet.   *He remains <u>in the city</u>.*

ABLATIVE OF PLACE FROM WHICH – Place *from which* is expressed by the ablative with the preposition ā/ab, dē or ē/ex.

<u>Ex urbe</u> venit.   *He comes <u>from the city</u>.*

INTRANSITIVE VERBS

INTRANSITIVE VERBS are verbs that cannot take a direct object. These often are used with a prepositional phrase.

In terrā vir <u>stat</u>.   *The man <u>stands</u> on the land.*

Vocabulary XXIV

Prepositions Followed by the Ablative		1ˢᵗ Conjugation Intransitive Verb (like **amō**)				
ā / ab	*from, away from; by*	stō,	stāre,	stetī	statum	*stand*
cum	*with, along with*					
dē	*about, concerning; down from*					
ē / ex	*from, out of*					
in	*in, on*	2ⁿᵈ Conjugation Intransitive Verbs (like **moneō**)				
prō	*in front of; on behalf of*	maneō,	manēre,	mānsī,	mānsum	*remain, stay*
sine	*without*	sedeō,	sedēre,	sēdī,	sessum	*sit*
sub	*under*					

Exercise XXIV

A.

1. Puerī cum pīrātā nōn manent.
2. Dux cum rēgīnā prō magnā et altā urbe sedēbat.
3. Corpus sine capite in mūrō stābit.
4. Nāvis longa sub aquā manēbat.
5. Nōmina filiārum filiōrumque nūntiata sunt.
6. Poētae in campō stābunt et carmina cantābunt.
7. Librī dē agrīs in ātrās silvās ab agricolīs portātī erunt.
8. Parva puella sine nōmine in urbe errat.
9. Malus pīrāta parvōs puerōs tēlō terruerit.
10. Piōs filiōs ad bellum in urbe pīrātārum dūximus.
11. Pectus mīlitis tēlīs agricolārum vulnerātum est.
12. Iūra rēgīnārum ab cīvibus urbium accepta sunt.
13. Magister amīcam epistulam dē lēgibus ad parvum puerum mittet.
14. Incolae urbium ad nāvīs pulchrās in lītore iter faciunt.
15. In silvā sedēbātis, quod fessī erātis.
16. Scrība longa carmina dē ducibus gentium scrīpserat.

B.

1. The body of the sailor will remain on the coast in front of the city.
2. The ships of the angry queen had fled from the city.
3. I was hearing the songs about the ships in my sleep.
4. You (sg.) had sat in the ship on the sea with the little girls.
5. You (pl.) were wandering out of the fields and singing songs without books.
6. The beautiful sister of the little girl was standing in front of the angry soldier.
7. The tribe of pirates had remained in the city with the leader.
8. The gates of the city were guarded by the inhabitants with weapons.
9. The evil citizens will not remain with their sons in the city.
10. We captured the evil men with the sacred weapons of the gods.
11. My heart has been wounded by the words of the leaders.
12. The long river sends ships of the native land into the great, black sea.

Lesson XXV

THIRD DECLENSION ADJECTIVES

Many adjectives use endings of the third declension.

To find the stem remove the ending from the genitive singular.

A few third declension adjectives have a masculine singular ending in **-er**. These adjectives have a different form in the nominative singular for each gender.

- The ablative singular of all genders ends in **-ī**   ĀCRIS
- The genitive plural of all genders ends in **-ium**   ___-IS___
- The accusative plural masculine and feminine end in **-īs**   ĀCR-
- The nominative and accusative plural neuter end in **-ia**

ADJECTIVES OF THREE TERMINATIONS

Singular	Masculine		Feminine		Neuter	
Nominative	ācer		ācris		ācre	
Genitive	ācris		ācris		ācris	
Dative	ācrī		ācrī		ācrī	
Accusative	ācrem		ācrem		ācre	
Ablative	ācrī	←	ācrī	←	ācrī	←
Plural						
Nominative	ācrēs		ācrēs		ācria	←
Genitive	ācrium	←	ācrium	←	ācrium	←
Dative	ācribus		ācribus		ācribus	
Accusative	ācrīs	←	ācrīs	←	ācria	←
Ablative	ācribus		ācribus		ācribus	

USES OF ADJECTIVES

The **ATTRIBUTIVE** use of adjectives gives information about the noun modified.

> Puella <u>pulchra</u> cantat.   *The <u>beautiful</u> girl is singing.*

The **PREDICATIVE** use of adjectives follows a linking verb and completes the meaning of the sentence.

> Mīles est <u>amīcus</u>.   *The soldier is <u>friendly</u>.*

The **SUBSTANTIVE** use of adjectives: Adjectives are often used without nouns in Latin; the gender of the adjectives signifies "men," "women," or "things."

masculine:	**bonus**	= *a good man*	**bonī**	= *good men*
feminine:	**bona**	= *a good woman*	**bonae**	= *good women*
neuter:	**bonum**	= *a good thing*	**bona**	= *good things/ goods*

> <u>Bonī</u> deōs laudant.   <u>*Good people*</u> *praise the gods.*

50

Vocabulary XXV

3rd Declension Nouns				3rd Declension Adjectives (like ācer)			
lux,	lūcis,	f.	*light*	ācer,	ācris,	ācre	*sharp, fierce, keen*
nox,	noctis,	f.	*night*	celer,	celeris,	celere	*swift, quick*
mons,	montis,	m.	*mountain*	2nd Declension Nouns (like **verbum**)			
pons,	pontis,	m.	*bridge*	regnum,	regnī,	n.	*kingdom*

Exercise XXV

A.

1. Nostrōs capient.
2. Prō rēgnō pugnābitis.
3. Puella pulchra in ponte sēdit.
4. Celerēs ā mūrō fugiunt.
5. Cum amīcīs manēbāmus.
6. Lux in monte erat pulchra.
7. Rēgīna ex rēgnō nōn veniet.
8. Celer ventus dē montibus vēnit.
9. Sine īrā celer servus fūgit.
10. Nōmen rēgnī nostrī est magnum.
11. Miserae verba sacra deī audiēbant et pectora mūniēbant.
12. Celerēs ācrēsque laudātae sunt.
13. Puerī aegrī tēlīs, nōn verbīs, vulnerātī erant.
14. Līberī ē terrā marīque itinera faciunt.
15. Servī in agrīs manent et prō agricolīs opera faciunt.
16. Ācria verba dominī in pectoribus nostrīs tenēbimus.

B.

1. of the swift soldiers
2. by sharp words
3. toward many mountains
4. into the dark woods
5. under the high bridge
6. about the great body
7. by my teacher
8. on behalf of the slaves
9. out of night
10. without anger
11. She had been wounded in the head by a sharp weapon.
12. Night flees with the light.
13. Good people teach boys and girls by (their) deeds.
14. Your head will remain on your body.
15. We have received many songs and letters.
16. The sons and daughters of our native land have been called into the city.
17. You (sg.) will be praised because you have not been mistaken.
18. The tired soldiers carried burdens out of the water and onto the bridge.

Lesson XXVI

THIRD DECLENSION ADJECTIVES

Some third declension adjectives have only two forms for the nominative singular: one for the masculine and feminine, and one for the neuter.

To find the stem remove the ending from the genitive singular.

$$\begin{array}{r} \text{OMNIS} \\ \underline{\text{-IS}} \\ \text{OMN-} \end{array}$$

ADJECTIVES OF TWO TERMINATIONS

Singular	Masculine/Feminine	Neuter
Nominative	omnis	omne
Genitive	omnis	omnis
Dative	omnī	omnī
Accusative	omnem	omne
Ablative	omnī	omnī
Plural		
Nominative	omnēs	omnia
Genitive	omnium	omnium
Dative	omnibus	omnibus
Accusative	omnīs (ēs)	omnia
Ablative	omnibus	omnibus

Some third declension adjectives have only one nominative singular form. This is used with masculine, feminine, and neuter nouns.

The dictionary forms of these words are given as with nouns: the nominative singular and genitive singular: e.g. fēlīx, fēlīcis.

ADJECTIVES OF ONE TERMINATION

Singular	Masculine/Feminine	Neuter
Nominative	fēlīx	fēlīx
Genitive	fēlīcis	fēlīcis
Dative	fēlīcī	fēlīcī
Accusative	fēlīcem	fēlīx
Ablative	fēlīcī	fēlīcī
Plural		
Nominative	fēlīcēs	fēlīcia
Genitive	fēlīcium	fēlīcium
Dative	fēlīcibus	fēlīcibus
Accusative	fēlīcīs (ēs)	fēlīcia
Ablative	fēlīcibus	fēlīcibus

IRREGULAR THIRD DECLENSION NOUNS

The nouns **māter**, **pater**, and **frāter**, though parisyllabic, are not i-stems and have a genitive plural ending **-um**.

māt**rum**   *of the mothers*   pat**rum**   *of the fathers*   frāt**rum**   *of the brothers*

Vocabulary XXVI

3rd Declension Adjectives (like **omnis**)			Irregular 3rd Declension Nouns			
brevis,	breve	*short, brief*	frāter,	frātris,	m.	*brother*
omnis,	omne	*every, all*	māter,	matris,	f.	*mother*
3rd Declension Adjectives (like fēlīx)			pater,	patris,	m.	*father*
audax,	audācis	*bold*				
fēlīx	fēlīcis	*happy*				

Exercise XXVI

A.

1. Omnēs mātrem et patrem amant.
2. Tuus filius et nostra filia librōs brevīs tenēbant.
3. Audāx dominus carmina longa poētae magnī cantābit.
4. Fēlīcēs frātrēs ā puellīs vocābantur.
5. Māter pīrātae umbrās brevīs in silvīs vīderat.
6. Puerōs ācrīs dē marī et nāvibus docueritis.
7. Magnum pectus mīlitis tēlīs ducis celeris vulnerātum est.
8. Altī montēs ātrās silvās et flūmina longa tenēbunt.
9. Amīca soror rēgīnae parvum puerum portāverat, quod fessus erat.
10. Dominus bonus nuntium fēlīcem ad urbem mittit.
11. Pīrātae omnia facta mala nautārum in librīs et epistulīs laudābunt.
12. Magna onera gentis ab omnibus in ponte posita erant.

B.

1. The lights of all the cities remain.
2. All the citizens of the city came to the bridge.
3. The short and sharp words of the little boy will wound the mother and father.
4. The soldiers without weapons were wandering into the dark forests of the native land.
5. We sent the masters and slaves of the land to the queen.
6. The bridge of the city will remain because it will carry the soldiers to the forest.
7. The inhabitants of the mountain had seen many ghosts, but were not frightened.
8. The long river carries the happy sailors by ship to the sea.
9. The god of sleep led my brothers and sisters into the night.
10. The dutiful daughters will place the books and letters onto the walls.
11. Mothers and fathers wandered out of the forests and into the cities of the kingdom.
12. The bold little boys wounded every soldier of the tribe with sharp weapons.

Lesson XXVII

SECOND CONJUGATION: Ē-VERBS
Present System Passive Voice

The personal endings are the same as the First Conjugation.

PRESENT TENSE

Singular		
1st person	mone**or**	*I am (being) warned*
2nd person	mon**ēris**	*you are (being) warned*
3rd person	mon**ētur**	*he/she/it is (being) warned*
Plural		
1st person	mon**ēmur**	*we are (being) warned*
2nd person	mon**ēminī**	*you are (being) warned*
3rd person	mone**ntur**	*they are (being) warned*

IMPERFECT TENSE

Singular			
1st person	monē**bar**	*I was being warned,*	*-used to be warned*
2nd person	monē**bāris**	*you were being warned,*	*-used to be warned*
3rd person	monē**bātur**	*he/she/it was being warned,*	*-used to be warned*
Plural			
1st person	monē**bāmur**	*we were being warned,*	*-used to be warned*
2nd person	monē**bāminī**	*you were being warned,*	*-used to be warned*
3rd person	monē**bantur**	*they were being warned,*	*-used to be warned*

FUTURE TENSE

Singular		
1st person	monē**bor**	*I will be warned*
2nd person	monē**beris**	*you will be warned*
3rd person	monē**bitur**	*he/she/it will be warned*
Plural		
1st person	monē**bimur**	*we will be warned*
2nd person	monē**biminī**	*you will be warned*
3rd person	monē**buntur**	*they will be warned*

APPOSITION

A noun describing another noun is an **APPOSITIVE**. An appositive agrees in case with the noun it modifies.

Gāius <u>rex</u> pugnāvit.   *Gaius <u>the king</u> has fought.*

Gāium <u>regem</u> timēmus. *We fear Gaius <u>the king</u>.*

Est fīlius Gāiī <u>regis</u>. *He is the son of Gaius <u>the king</u>.*

54

Vocabulary XXVII

2nd Conjugation Verbs (like **moneō**)					3rd Declension Noun (like **mīles**)			
moveō,	movēre,	mōvī,	mōtum	*move*	rex,	regis,	m.	*king*
dēleō,	dēlēre,	dēlēvī,	dēlētum	*destroy*				

Exercise XXVII

A.

1. Omnis urbs dēlēbitur.
2. Patrēs fēlīcēs videntur.
3. Porta nōn movētur.
4. Verba docentur.
5. Caput meum teneō.

6. Māter mea, rēgīna magna, amātur.
7. Frāter tuus, poēta fēlīx, librum scrīpsit.
8. Fīliī fīliaeque ā magistrō bonō monēbantur.
9. Ācer rex in orā regnī sedēbat.
10. Cīvis bonus lūcem nōn timuit.

11. Incolae terrae verbīs piīs regis bonī movēbuntur.
12. Celeris nox dē montibus ad mare vēnit.
13. Audāx soror cum frātribus multa bella pugnābat.
14. Miserī mīlitēs corpora ex flūmine in terram mōverant.
15. Īra magna rēgīnae ab omnibus cīvibus vīsa est.
16. Tua fīlia, mea amīca, carmina poētārum amat, sed nōn librōs.
17. Lēgēs regnī ā scrībā, meō frātre, dēlentur.
18. Puella ā magistrō laudāta est quod īram tenuerat.

B.

1. The city will be destroyed.
2. Our leader, a bold man, has been praised.
3. My books are being moved.
4. Water is being carried.
5. You (pl.) will have been wounded.
6. We had been asked by the king.
7. The inhabitants of the native land will be moved.
8. The farmers, the leaders of the tribe, will be angry.
9. You will be seen by my brother on the playing field.
10. The tired men, your brothers, are sitting under the bridge.
11. The citizens killed the queen because she had led the poets out of the native land.
12. Gaius, the slave, has written many books and many letters on behalf of my father.

Lesson XXVIII

SECOND CONJUGATION: Ē-VERBS
Perfect System Passive Voice

The passive voice of the perfect system is formed in the same way for all verbs: the fourth principal part, declined like **bonus**, is followed by the appropriate form of **sum**.

PERFECT TENSE

Singular			
1st person	monitus / -a sum	*I was advised,*	*-have been advised*
2nd person	monitus / -a es	*you were advised,*	*-have been advised*
3rd person	monitus / -a / -um est	*he/she/it was advised,*	*-has been advised*
Plural			
1st person	monitī / -ae sumus	*we were advised,*	*-have been advised*
2nd person	monitī / -ae estis	*you were advised,*	*-have been advised*
3rd person	monitī / -ae / -a sunt	*they were advised,*	*-have been advised*

PLUPERFECT TENSE

Singular		
1st person	monitus / -a eram	*I had been advised*
2nd person	monitus / -a erās	*you had been advised*
3rd person	monitus / -a / -um erat	*he/she/it had been advised*
Plural		
1st person	monitī / -ae erāmus	*we had been advised*
2nd person	monitī / -ae erātis	*you had been advised*
3rd person	monitī / -ae / -a erant	*they had been advised*

FUTURE PERFECT TENSE

Singular		
1st person	monitus / -a erō	*I will have been advised*
2nd person	monitus / -a eris	*you will have been advised*
3rd person	monitus / -a / -um erit	*he/she/it will have been advised*
Plural		
1st person	monitī / -ae erimus	*we will have been advised*
2nd person	monitī / -ae eritis	*you will have been advised*
3rd person	monitī / -ae / -a erunt	*they will have been advised*

ABLATIVE OF TIME WHEN

ABLATIVE OF TIME WHEN OR WITHIN WHICH: Latin uses the ablative case with no preposition to express the time when or within which something happens. English uses various prepositions: *on, at, in, during, by,* and occasionally no preposition.

<u>Proximō annō</u> Caesar urbem dēlēvit.   *<u>(In the) next year</u> Caesar destroyed the city.*

Vocabulary XXVIII

3rd Conjugation Verbs (like **dūcō**)					2nd Declension Nouns (like **dominus**)			
dīcō,	dīcere,	dīxī,	dictum	*say, speak, tell*	annus,	annī,	m.	*year*
regō,	regere,	rēxī,	rēctum	*rule*				
1st and 2nd Declension Adjectives (like bonus)					**1st Declension Nouns (like puella)**			
prīmus,	prīma,	prīmum		*first*	hōra,	hōrae,	f.	*hour*
proximus,	proxima,	proximum		*next*	prīmā lūce			*at dawn*

Exercise XXVIII

A.

1. Gentēs miserae rēctae sunt.
2. Mīlitēs audācēs laudātī erant.
3. Soror mea prīmā hōrā docta est.
4. Nōmina mīlitum proximō annō nūntiāta erunt.
5. Fīliī tēlō nōn territī erant.
6. Urbs dēlēta erat et cīvēs pūnītī erant.
7. Ad rēgīnam vocātus erās.
8. Vulnerātī sumus.
9. Verbīs tuīs mōtus sum.
10. Nostrae sorōris vōx est pulchra.
11. In lītore manēbitis.
12. Sub ponte in flūmine stetistī.

13. Nocte prō portīs stābis et cīvīs servābis.
14. Prō duce fēlīcia carmina cantābō.
15. Pīrātae malī ab rēgnō fūgērunt et iter ad mare fēcērunt.
16. Brevī nocte iter ad montēs faciēmus et incolās monēbimus.
17. Prīmā lūce parābiminī quod mīlitēs vīderimus.
18. Corpora dē montibus portāvimus et in nāvīs cum capitibus posuimus.
19. Prīmā hōrā īrāta gēns multa misera dīxit.
20. Proximō annō multōs mūrōs Rōmae mūnīvimus.
21. Omnēs lēgēs in pectoribus nostrīs tenēbuntur.
22. Prīmā hōrā in ponte stābāmus et flūmen vidēbāmus.

B.

1. Your hearts have not been moved.
2. Our native land had been destroyed by night.
3. The queen's anger will have been reported.
4. We will rule with your (sg.) friends.
5. You (sg.) will come at dawn.
6. We are not killing sick soldiers.

7. I love all the songs of my native land.
8. Next year he will see my brother on a high mountain.
9. You (pl.) were seen under the bridge with the daughter of the king.
10. The father and mother will have been saved by our slaves.
11. I will take the letters from the messenger and carry (them) to the king.
12. In the first year of the war all the inhabitants were frightened by the deeds of bad (men).

Lesson XXIX

FOURTH DECLENSION NOUNS

Nouns whose genitive singular ends in **-ūs** belong to the FOURTH DECLENSION.

To find the stem of any Latin noun, remove the ending from the genitive singular.

GRADŪS	CORNŪS
-ŪS	-ŪS
GRAD-	CORN-

Most fourth declension nouns are masculine. A few fourth declension nouns are neuter and have a nominative ending in **-ū.**

Fourth declension nouns are declined by adding the case endings to the noun stem: **grad-** or **corn-**

Fourth declension feminine nouns use the same endings as the masculine.

Singular	ending			
Nominative	**-us**	→	grad**us**	*step*
Genitive	**-ūs**	→	grad**ūs**	*of the step, step's*
Dative	**-uī**	→	grad**uī**	*to / for the step*
Accusative	**-um**	→	grad**um**	*step*
Ablative	**-ū**	→	grad**ū**	*by / with / from the step*
Plural				
Nominative	**-ūs**	→	grad**ūs**	*steps*
Genitive	**-uum**	→	grad**uum**	*of the steps*
Dative	**-ibus**	→	grad**ibus**	*to / for the steps*
Accusative	**-ūs**	→	grad**ūs**	*steps*
Ablative	**-ibus**	→	grad**ibus**	*by / with / from the steps*

- If the nominative singular of the noun ends in **-ū**, the noun is neuter in gender.

Singular	ending			
Nominative	**-ū**	→	corn**ū**	*horn*
Genitive	**-ūs**	→	corn**ūs**	*of the horn, horn's*
Dative	**-ū**	→	corn**ū**	*to / for the horn*
Accusative	**-ū**	→	corn**ū**	*horn*
Ablative	**-ū**	→	corn**ū**	*by / with / from the horn*
Plural				
Nominative	**-ua**	→	corn**ua**	*horns*
Genitive	**-uum**	→	corn**uum**	*of the horns*
Dative	**-ibus**	→	corn**ibus**	*to / for the horns*
Accusative	**-ūa**	→	corn**ūa**	*horns*
Ablative	**-ibus**	→	corn**ibus**	*by / with / from the horns*

Vocabulary XXIX

4th Declension Nouns (like **gradus** or **cornū**)				3rd Declension Adjective (like **omnis**)		
cāsus,	cāsūs,	m.	*chance, misfortune, fall*	fortis,	forte	*brave, strong*
domus,	domūs,	f.	*home, household* *			
exercitus,	exercitūs,	m.	*army*			
fluctus,	fluctūs,	m.	*wave, tide, flood; (pl.) sea*			
gradus,	gradūs,	m.	*step*			
manus,	manūs,	f.	*hand*			
cornū	cornūs,	n.	*horn*			

*<u>Domus</u> often uses ablative **domō**.

Exercise XXIX

A.

1. Flūctūs maris in meō somnō audiō.
2. Ātra est prīma hōra noctis.
3. Exercitus patriae in dominōs in silvā pugnābat.
4. Proximō annō rēgīna cāsūs agricolārum miserōrum vīdit.
5. Omnēs domūs urbis flūctibus marium dēlēbuntur.
6. Deī deaeque maris, nōn nautae, fluctūs regunt.
7. Gradūs parvārum filiārum ab fēlīcī mātre laudātī sunt.
8. Cornua in portīs domūs posuērunt.
9. Magnae navēs ab dominō et bonīs servīs nōn movēbantur.
10. Magister puerōrum multa verba et pulchrōs librōs docuerat.
11. Prīmā lūce īrātus pater mīlitis miserī multa verba dīxit.
12. Mīlitēs pontem mūnīverant quod flūmen erat altum.
13. Cornū magnō rēgīna domum omnem vocāvit.
14. Manibus pectoribusque mīlitum fortium cīvēs servābuntur.

B.

1. Horns are weapons of the inhabitants of forests.
2. The waves of the dark sea will not frighten the brave king.
3. The pirates and sailors led the boys and mothers from the homes.
4. I prepared our great ships and led the sailors onto the shore in the night.
5. The sharp words of the angry ghosts terrify the tired girls of the city.
6. You (sg.) had wandered into the forests and fields without your books.
7. With large waves the swift seas carried the tall ships to the shore.
8. The brave soldiers had not asked the beautiful queen about the next war.
9. We will have held the books and letters of the holy poet in our hands.
10. The words of all the poets will have been written by hand.

Lesson XXX

THIRD CONJUGATION: CONSONANT AND I-STEM VERBS
Present System Passive Voice

PRESENT TENSE

Singular					
1st person	dūcor	*I am (being) led*	capior	*I am (being) captured*
2nd person	dūceris	*you are (being) led*	caperis ←	*you are (being) captured*
3rd person	dūcitur	*he/she/it is (being) led*	capitur	*he/she/it is (being) captured*
Plural					
1st person	dūcimur	*we are (being) led*	capimur	*we are (being) captured*
2nd person	dūciminī	*you are (being) led*	capiminī	*you are (being) captured*
3rd person	dūcuntur	*they are (being) led*	capiuntur	*they are (being) captured*

IMPERFECT TENSE

Singular					
1st person	dūcēbar	*I was being led*	capiēbar	*I was being captured*
2nd person	dūcēbāris	*you were being led*	capiēbāris	*you were being captured*
3rd person	dūcēbātur	*he/she/it was being led*	capiēbātur	*he/she/it was being captured*
Plural					
1st person	dūcēbāmur	*we were being led*	capiēbāmur	*we were being captured*
2nd person	dūcēbāminī	*you were being led*	capiēbāminī	*you were being captured*
3rd person	dūcēbantur	*they were being led*	capiēbantur	*they were being captured*

FUTURE TENSE

Singular					
1st person	dūcar	*I will be led*	capiar	*I shall be captured*
2nd person	dūcēris	*you will be led*	capiēris	*you will be captured*
3rd person	dūcētur	*he/she/it will be led*	capiētur	*he/she/it will be captured*
Plural					
1st person	dūcēmur	*we will be led*	capiēmur	*we shall be captured*
2nd person	dūcēminī	*you will be led*	capiēminī	*you will be captured*
3rd person	dūcentur	*they will be led*	capientur	*they will be captured*

- In the third conjugation the future tense is marked by vowels.
- I-stem verbs have an **-i-** in every form of the present passive system except the present tense, second person singular.

ACCUSATIVE OF DURATION OF TIME

Latin uses noun phrases in the accusative case with no preposition to express how long an action lasts. English often uses the preposition *for* or no preposition.

> Multōs annōs rex regēbat.   *The king ruled <u>for many years</u>.*
>
> Multōs annōs in Ītaliā manēbimus.   *We will stay in Italy <u>many years</u>.*

Vocabulary XXX

3rd Conjugation Verbs (like **dūcō**)				
cernō,	cernere,	crēvī,	crētum	*perceive, discern*
gerō,	gerere,	gessī,	gestum	*carry on;* (bellum gerere, *wage war*)
volvō,	volvere,	volvī,	volūtum	*roll*
tegō,	tegere,	texī,	tectum	*cover, conceal, shelter*
3rd Declension Adjectives (like **omnis**)				
dulcis,	dulce	*sweet*		
gravis,	grave	*heavy; serious*		

Exercise XXX

A.

1. Amīcī ā dominīs cernuntur.
2. Multa bella gerēbantur.
3. Silvīs tegēmur.
4. Multās hōrās dīcēbātis.
5. Regnum ā rēgibus malīs multōs annōs regēbātur.
6. Flūctūs altō marī ad lītus volvuntur.
7. Prīmā hōrā bellum gerētur et urbēs dēlēbuntur.
8. Mīlitēs ex exercitū ā gravī dūce mōtī erunt.
9. Ab amīcīs nostrīs cernēbāmur.
10. Soror mea īrāta prō rēge stetit et multa verba dīxit.
11. Celer ventus et flūctūs magnī nāvīs nostrās ad ōram mīsērunt.
12. Mare magnum et celerēs ventī nāvem vestram in terram volvent.
13. Multōs annōs fessī mīlitēs itinera faciēbant et bella pugnābant.
14. Māter dulcis rēgīnae in ponte stābat et ā cīvibus laudābātur.
15. Pīrātās nōn vīdimus quod mare ātrā nocte tegēbātur.
16. Poēta carmina dē incolīs patriae sed nōn dē rēge nostrō scrīpsit.

B.

1. For many years bold slaves were waging war with (their) masters.
2. The happy sailors have perceived friendly girls on the shore.
3. The names of the sweet girls will be written in books.
4. The gods will punish the black heart of the evil king for all (his) years.
5. The soldier's body had been watched over by (his) loyal friends.
6. The sailors' bodies were being rolled over by the waves of the river.
7. You (sg.) will discern the voice of the god on the holy mountain.
8. Brave men were being sheltered in our house for the first hour.
9. In the next hour the words of your leaders will be reported.
10. During the night the heavy walls of the city were being destroyed by the soldiers.
11. The heavy steps of the angry queen are being perceived by the king.
12. For many years the devoted king was carrying the burdens of all the citizens.

Lesson XXXI

THIRD CONJUGATION: CONSONANT AND I-STEM VERBS
Perfect System Passive Voice

The passive voice of the perfect system is formed the same way for all verbs: the fourth principal part, declined like **bonus** is followed by the appropriate form of **sum**.

PERFECT TENSE

Singular			
1st person	ductus / -a sum	*I was led,*	*-have been led*
2nd person	ductus / -a es	*you were led,*	*-have been led*
3rd person	ductus / -a / -um est	*he/she/it was led,*	*-has been led*
Plural			
1st person	ductī / -ae sumus	*we were led,*	*-have been led*
2nd person	ductī / -ae estis	*you were led,*	*-have been led*
3rd person	ductī / -ae / -a sunt	*they were led,*	*-have been led*

PLUPERFECT TENSE

Singular		
1st person	ductus / -a eram	*I had been led*
2nd person	ductus / -a erās	*you had been led*
3rd person	ductus / -a / -um erat	*he/she/it had been led*
Plural		
1st person	ductī / -ae erāmus	*we had been led*
2nd person	ductī / -ae erātis	*you had been led*
3rd person	ductī / -ae / -a erant	*they had been led*

FUTURE PERFECT TENSE

Singular		
1st person	ductus / -a erō	*I will have been led*
2nd person	ductus / -a eris	*you will have been led*
3rd person	ductus / -a / -um erit	*he/she/it will have been led*
Plural		
1st person	ductī / -ae erimus	*we will have been led*
2nd person	ductī / -ae eritis	*you will have been led*
3rd person	ductī / -ae / -a erunt	*they will have been led*

THE DATIVE CASE

DATIVE CASE is used for **INDIRECT OBJECTS**. An indirect object is a person to or for whom something is given, said, told or shown.

    Librōs <u>puellae</u> monstrō.   *I show <u>the girl</u> the books; I show the books <u>to the girl</u>.*

The dative case is used with some adjectives.

    Liber ūtilis <u>magistrō</u> est.   *The book is useful <u>to the teacher</u>.*
    Verba poētae sunt similia <u>carminī</u>.   *The poet's words are like <u>a song</u>.*

Vocabulary XXXI

	Irregular Verb				1st and 2nd Declension Adjectives (like **bonus**)			
dō,	dare,	dedī,	datum	*say, speak, tell*	cārus,	cāra,	cārum	*dear*
3rd Declension Adjectives (like **omnis**)					2nd Declension Nouns (like **verbum**)			
similis,	simile	*similar, like (+ dative)*			dōnum,	dōnī,	n.	*gift*
ūtilis,	ūtile	*useful*						

Exercise XXXI

A.

1. Magister librum parvae puellae dat.
2. Epistulās longās nūntiīs nōn dabāmus.
3. Agrī patriae dominīs agricolīsque datī erant.
4. Dōna rēgīnārum fēlīcibus puerīs dabuntur.
5. Scrībae fuērunt ūtilēs poētīs quod librōs scrīpsērunt.
6. Liber epistulaque sunt ūtilēs magistrō.
7. Parvae puellae urbis magnae erunt cārae deae.
8. Onera gravia mīlitum ā servīs rēgīnae dulcis portāta erant.
9. Deī deaeque pulchrōs campōs umbrīs ātrīs noctis tēxērunt.
10. Nautae ex marī altōs montīs et omnīs domūs patriae cernunt.
11. Fluctūs magnī flūminis navīs volvent et audācīs pīrātās terrēbunt.
12. Lux in domō ātrā est similis dōnō deōrum.

B.

1. The little boys are dear to (their) brothers, the soldiers.
2. The short hours of the night are useful to all.
3. The words of our teacher are like the words of the gods.
4. War is bad for all the tribes of our native land.
5. The farmers from the fields are giving gifts to the pirates of the seas.
6. The beautiful book of the poets has been sent to the teacher of my daughters.
7. My sister, the queen, gives letters to the messenger, and the soldiers guard the gates.
8. Because the strong mother guards (her) sons and daughters, she is like a soldier.
9. The rights of citizens were seized from the miserable farmers and slaves.
10. The slaves were sent into the dark forests for many years.
11. The great, holy books of the goddesses had been received by the happy citizens.
12. The inhabitants of the plain gave gifts to the sweet queen in the great city.

Lesson XXXII

FIFTH DECLENSION NOUNS

Nouns whose genitive singular ends in **-eī** belong to the **FIFTH DECLENSION**.

Fifth declension nouns are feminine in gender, except **diēs**, which is usually masculine.

To find the stem of any Latin noun, remove the ending from the genitive singular.

$$REĪ$$
$$\underline{-EĪ}$$
$$R-$$

Singular	ending			
Nominative	**-ēs**	→	**rēs**	*thing*
Genitive	**-eī***	→	**reī**	*of the thing, thing's*
Dative	**-eī***	→	**reī**	*to / for the step*
Accusative	**-em**	→	**rem**	*step*
Ablative	**-ē**	→	**rē**	*by / with / from the step*
Plural				
Nominative	**-ēs**	→	**rēs**	*things*
Genitive	**-ērum**	→	**rērum**	*of the things, things'*
Dative	**-ēbus**	→	**rēbus**	*to / for the things*
Accusative	**-ēs**	→	**rēs**	*things*
Ablative	**-ēbus**	→	**rēbus**	*by / with / from the things*

*The genitive and dative singular ending changes to **-ēī** when it is preceded by a vowel: **diēs** – gen. sg. **diēī**.

REVIEW OF THE CASE ENDINGS FOR THE FIVE DECLENSIONS

Singular	1st	2nd m.	2nd n.	3rd m. + f.	3rd n.	4th m. + f.	4th n.	5th f.
Nominative	**-a**	**-us**	**-um**	—	—	**-us**	**-ū**	**-ēs**
Genitive	**-ae**	**-ī**	**-ī**	**-is**	**-is**	**-ūs**	**-ūs**	**-eī**
Dative	**-ae**	**-ō**	**-ō**	**-ī**	**-ī**	**-uī**	**-ū**	**-eī**
Accusative	**-am**	**-um**	**-um**	**-em**	—	**-um**	**-ū**	**-em**
Ablative	**-ā**	**-ō**	**-ō**	**-e**	**-e/-ī**	**-ū**	**-ū**	**-ē**
Plural								
Nominative	**-ae**	**-ī**	**-a**	**-ēs**	**-a/ia**	**-ūs**	**-ua**	**-ēs**
Genitive	**-ārum**	**-ōrum**	**-ōrum**	**-um/ium**	**-um/ium**	**-uum**	**-uum**	**-ērum**
Dative	**-īs**	**-īs**	**-īs**	**-ibus**	**-ibus**	**-ibus**	**-ibus**	**-ēbus**
Accusative	**-ās**	**-ōs**	**-a**	**-ēs**	**-a/ia**	**-ūs**	**-ua**	**-ēs**
Ablative	**-īs**	**-īs**	**-īs**	**-ibus**	**-ibus**	**-ibus**	**-ibus**	**-ēbus**

Vocabulary XXXII

	5th Declension Nouns (like **rēs**)			3rd Declension Adjective (like **omnis**)		
diēs,	diēī,	m.	*day*	facilis,	facile	*easy*
fidēs,	fideī,	f.	*faith, loyalty*	difficilis,	difficile	*difficult*
rēs,	reī,	f.	*thing, affair, matter*			
speciēs,	speciēī,	f.	*appearance, sight*			
spēs,	speī,	f.	*hope*			

Exercise XXXII

A.

1. Mala fidēs incolārum regnum dēlēvit.
2. Rēs difficilēs, verba facilia sunt.
3. Spēs rēgīnae agricolīs et dominīs nuntiātae sunt, sed nōn pīrātīs et nautīs īrātīs.
4. Facilia facta fēlīcem virum piumque nōn facient.
5. Difficilem diem vīdistis, quod onera montibus similia portāvistis.
6. Rēs difficilīs exercitus faciet, quod mīlitēs audācēs sunt.
7. Prīmō diē nautae speciē corporum terrēbantur.
8. Prīma lux est brevis et pulchra hōra, sed incolae manent in somnō.
9. Rēgīnae patriae librōs et dōna omnī filiae dulcī dabunt, quod rēs difficilīs fēcerint.
10. Poētae et magistrī in terrīs cum frātribus et sorōribus errābant.
11. Scrība iter in urbem faciet, et audiet verba poētārum amīcōrum in ponte.
12. Vox vestrae filiae bonum patrem ad nāvem nōn vocāverat, sed in ōram.
13. Spē ventī nautae nāvēs altās parābunt.
14. Gradūs nuntiōrum parvī sunt, sed gradūs ducis parvī nōn sunt.

B.

1. The sweet queen was guarding the affairs of the city.
2. Hope of many good things will lead the citizens to war.
3. On the next day heavy burdens had been carried to my great ships on the seacoast.
4. We will have advised the bold leader about the evil hopes of angry pirates.
5. Faith is easy for the loyal heart, difficult for the evil (one).
6. You (sg.) sat on the high mountains for many days and sang about the affairs of the city.
7. The deeds of the man will show everyone the rights of the citizens.
8. The father had given the teacher (his) son's easy work.
9. The difficult sea used to be feared by the farmers and soldiers but not by the sailors and pirates.
10. The long songs of the poets wounded the king with sharp words.
11. The words of the sweet little girl are like songs and will move my great father.
12. The faith of our fathers will be destroyed by the appearance of the ghost at night.

Lesson XXXIII

FOURTH CONJUGATION: Ī-VERBS
Present System Passive Voice

PRESENT TENSE

Singular		
1st person	aud**ior**	*I am (being) heard*
2nd person	aud**īris**	*you are (being) heard*
3rd person	aud**ītur**	*he/she/it is (being) heard*
Plural		
1st person	aud**īmur**	*we are (being) heard*
2nd person	aud**īminī**	*you are (being) heard*
3rd person	aud**iuntur**	*they are (being) heard*

IMPERFECT TENSE

Singular			
1st person	aud**iēbar**	*I was being heard,*	*-used to be heard*
2nd person	aud**iēbāris**	*you were being heard,*	*-used to be heard*
3rd person	aud**iēbātur**	*he/she/it was being heard,*	*-used to be heard*
Plural			
1st person	aud**iēbāmur**	*we were being heard,*	*-used to be heard*
2nd person	aud**iēbāminī**	*you were being heard,*	*-used to be heard*
3rd person	aud**iēbantur**	*they were being heard,*	*-used to be heard*

FUTURE TENSE

Singular		
1st person	aud**iar**	*I will be heard*
2nd person	aud**iēris**	*you will be heard*
3rd person	aud**iētur**	*he/she/it will be heard*
Plural		
1st person	aud**iēmur**	*we will be heard*
2nd person	aud**iēminī**	*you will be heard*
3rd person	aud**ientur**	*they will be heard*

- In the fourth conjugation the future tense is marked by vowels.

The final **-ī** of the present stem is shortened before a vowel.

Vocabulary XXXIII

3rd Conjugation Verbs (like **dūcō**)				
surgō,	surgere,	surrēxī,	surrēctum	*rise, swell, stretch upward*
tendō,	tendere,	tendī,	tensum/tentum	*extend, stretch out, proceed*
3rd Declension Adjectives (like **fēlīx**)			3rd Declension Adjectives (like **omnis**)	
ingens,	ingentis	*huge, vast*	tristis, triste	*sad*
sapiens,	sapientis	*wise*		

Exercise XXXIII

A.

1. Verba ducis audiēbantur.
2. Cīvēs malī pūnientur.
3. Ingēns mūrus urbis nostrae mūniēbātur.
4. Bonī manūs ad deōs tendunt.
5. Carmina tristium puellārum nōn audientur.
6. Sapiēns rex nōn errāverat.
7. Ā deō maris ingentēs fluctūs in nautās miserōs volvēbantur.
8. Terra nostra ā marī magnō ad montēs tendit.
9. Īra mea surrēxit quod meum frātrem interfēcerant.
10. Scrība fessus verba tristis virī accipit et in librō scrībit.
11. Bellum est mīlitibus difficile sed ducibus facile.
12. Tristis speciēs ingentis virī sorōrem meam terruit.
13. Lēgēs patriae sunt sapientēs, sed ā cīvibus nōn laudantur.
14. Verba sapientium in urbe nostrā audientur.
15. Proximō diē fortēs mīlitēs in bellum cornū vocātī sunt.
16. Amīcus servus ā dominō aegrō capiētur et pūniētur.
17. Brevī nocte nostrae domūs rēsque omnēs in montēs mōvēbuntur.
18. Dulcis rēgīna gravem cāsum timēbat, sed similis rēgī exercitum dūcēbat.

B.

1. We carried great and heavy burdens for many hours.
2. All the cities of our native land were being fortified by our (men).
3. The messenger was sent out of the city at the first hour.
4. At dawn all our possessions will be sent into the ships.
5. You (pl.) were being heard by Gaius, our friend, and by many citizens.
6. For many days we sat on the shore and stayed with the sad sailors.
7. You (sg.) will be taught by the words and deeds of your teachers.
8. The master will be punished because he has said many evil things to the loyal slaves.
9. The light of day has fled before the huge shadow of the night.
10. I wrote many books and letters with my (own) hand.
11. The leaders rose and stretched out their hands to the gods.

Lesson XXXIV

FOURTH CONJUGATION: Ī-VERBS
Perfect System Passive Voice

The passive voice of the perfect system is formed the same way for all verbs: the fourth principal part, declined like **bonus**, is followed by the appropriate form of **sum**.

PERFECT TENSE

Singular			
1st person	audītus / -a sum	I was heard,	-have been heard
2nd person	audītus / -a es	you were heard,	-have been heard
3rd person	audītus / -a / -um est	he/she/it was heard,	-has been heard
Plural			
1st person	audītī / -ae sumus	we were heard,	-have been heard
2nd person	audītī / -ae estis	you were heard,	-have been heard
3rd person	audītī / -ae / -a sunt	they were heard,	-have been heard

PLUPERFECT TENSE

Singular		
1st person	audītus / -a eram	I had been heard
2nd person	audītus / -a erās	you had been heard
3rd person	audītus / -a / -um erat	he/she/it had been heard
Plural		
1st person	audītī / -ae erāmus	we had been heard
2nd person	audītī / -ae erātis	you had been heard
3rd person	audītī / -ae / -a erant	they had been heard

FUTURE PERFECT TENSE

Singular		
1st person	audītus / -a erō	I will have been heard
2nd person	audītus / -a eris	you will have been heard
3rd person	audītus / -a / -um erit	he/she/it will have been heard
Plural		
1st person	audītī / -ae erimus	we will have been heard
2nd person	audītī / -ae eritis	you will have been heard
3rd person	audītī / -ae / -a erunt	they will have been heard

Exercise XXXIV

A.

1. Ingentēs montēs ex terrā surgent et tegētur lux diēī.
2. Magister sapiens omnīs parvōs puerōs in agrīs prīmā hōrā diēī docēbit.
3. Tristis liber dē rēge rēgīnāque ab duce mīlitibus datus est.
4. Umbrae silvae ad flūmen tendunt, sed prīmā lūce nōn vidēbuntur.
5. Urbs nostra nōn montibus et flūminibus mūnīta erat, sed spē et pectoribus cīvium fortium.
6. Epistulae longae mātrum et patrum ad filiās filiōsque missae erunt.
7. Nōmen agricolae audācis in omnī urbe patriae audītum est.
8. Ā duce fessō nōn pūnītī erāmus, sed multa mala fēcerāmus.
9. Dulcia carmina poētārum ā parvīs puerīs et puellīs cantāta sunt.
10. Īrāta soror rēgīnae prō portīs urbis cum audācī mīlite nocte stābit.
11. Longīs hōrīs noctis terrae umbrīs tēctae sunt et flūctūs ventīs volūtī sunt.
12. Amīcī incolae urbis fuērunt similēs fēlīcibus nautīs.
13. Difficilis liber ad bellum ā servīs ducis portātur.
14. Rēgīna, cāra rēgī bonō, ingentibus nāvibus pīrātārum malōrum territa est.
15. Portae ātrae domūs fortibus fluctibus et celeribus ventīs dēlētae erunt.
16. Ingēns īra deōrum et deārum fessōs cīvīs in silvās et agrōs mīserat.

B.

1. In the night the high bridge had been captured by the angry citizens.
2. The voice of the small leader was heard under water.
3. Our city has been fortified by the bodies of our brave citizens, not by walls and weapons.
4. The hearts of the boys and girls had been fortified by the words of a wise book.
5. Our sons will seize the books about the beautiful girls from the wall of the house.
6. The sweet voices of the holy goddesses were heard the next day from the mountains.
7. You (sg.) will be punished because you will have hurt the plains and fields of your native land.
8. We stayed on the ships because pirates were in the city.
9. The heavy burdens were placed on the wall of the city by the tired slaves.
10. Bad things have not been taught by your wise teacher.
11. The rights of citizens are similar to gifts of the gods.
12. We wrote a long letter to the queen, because you (sg.) had done many good deeds.
13. The misfortunes of the happy poets destroyed the faith of the bold citizens.
14. I had feared the angry voice of my father, but not the sweet gifts of my mother.
15. The hopes of the king were destroyed by the anger of the slaves.
16. The gift of the wise teacher will be useful to the sad girl.

Readings

The following short passages use primarily vocabulary and grammar from the lessons indicated. Additional vocabulary is given below the passage. The first passages are numbered as individual sentences, but seek to have some sequential sense. Later passages narrate succinctly the legends of Romulus and Remus, Tarquinius Superbus, Lucretia, the Horatii and Curiatii, Horatius at the Bridge, and the Dictatorship of Cincinnatus.

These passages are intended to be read in class, as sight translation, with the help and guidance of the teacher. The legends have been chosen to provide opportunities for general discussion of the development of Roman government, culture, and values.

Some unfamiliar words should be guessed with the help of English cognates; meanings of italicized words are given beneath each passage.

Lessons I - V

1. Agricola patriam amat.
2. Patria agricolam vocat.
3. Agricola *prō* patriā pugnāre parat.
4. Agricola prō patriā pugnat et patriam servat.
5. Patria agricolam laudat, *quod* patriam servāvit.
6. Poētae agricolam laudant et *dē* agricolā cantābunt.

prō	*on behalf of*
quod	*because*
dē	*about*

Lessons I - VI

1. Ītalia est longa paenīnsula in *marī*.
2. Rōma est *urbs maxima* in Ītaliā.
3. Rōmānī urbem Rōmam amant.
4. Rōmānī aquam amant; aqua Rōmānōs nōn terret.
5. Mare Rōmānōs *ad* Graeciam et ad Siciliam et ad Africam portat.
6. Rōmānī aquam "Mare Nostrum" vocant.
7. Rōmānī in marī errant, et aqua Rōmānōs nōn vulnerat.

marī	*sea*
urbs	*city*
maxima	*greatest*
ad	*to*

Lessons I - VIII

1. Magister librum tenet; librum portat.
2. Puellae librum vident et magistrum rogant,
3. "Librum*ne nōbis mōnstrābis?*"
4. "*Vōbis* librum mōnstrābō."
5. Magister puellās librōs amāre docet.
6. Magistrum puellae laudant et docēre parat.
7. *Subitō* puellae umbram vident; umbra puellās terret.
8. Magister īram nōn tenet.

-ne	*(particle indicating a question)*
nōbīs	*us*
mōnstrābis	*you will show*
vōbīs	*you*
subitō	*suddenly*

Lessons I - X

1. Magister puerōs vocat.
2. Puerī pūgnābant; magister īram nōn tenuit.
3. Puerī īram timent; nōn pugnābunt.
4. Magister dominum vīdit et puerōs monuit.
5. Puerī verba in librīs scrībunt; magister librum scrīpsit.
6. Dominus magistrum et puerōs laudābit.

Lessons I - XII

1. Agricolae agrōs servāre parābant.
2. Deam magnam laudāvērunt.
3. Magna dea aquam multam mittet.
4. Aqua agrōs nōn vulnerābit; agricolae bonam aquam et deam magnam nōn timent.
5. Agricolae bonī patriam et rēgīnam magnam amant.

Lessons I - XIV

1. In librīs poētae *dē* vīrīs et deīs scrīpsērunt.
2. Mercūrius, nuntius *deōrum*, veniet quod deī mīsērunt.
3. Nuntius virōs monēbit; virī audient et portās mūnient.
4. Virī pugnābunt et puellās puerōsque servābunt.
5. Deum laudābimus, quod virōs monuit et nostrōs filiōs filiāsque servāvit.

dē	*about*
deōrum	*(gen.) of the gods*

Fābula dē Rōmulō et Remō

Lessons I - XVI

Romans were fond of explaining their special role in the world as being due to the divine ancestry of the founder of Rome.

Multī deī Rōmānōs servābant; dē deīs poētae fābulās multās narrant. Deus Mars *erat* deus bellī; erat fīlius *Iovis*. Mars *ōlim* ad Rheam Silviam in somnō vēnit et fīliōs *geminōs* fēcērunt. Nōmina geminōrum erant Rōmulus Remusque. *Rēx malus* fīliōs timuit quod rēgnum ā *patre* Rheae Silviae cēperat. Rēx *putāvit*, "Fīliī Rheae Silviae erunt rēgēs." Rex *igitur* puerōs īnfantīs *in* silvās mīsit, sed Mars fīliōs servāvit. Mars *lupam* mīsit, *quae* Rōmulum et Remum *nūtrīvit*. Puerī lupam nōn timuērunt et nōn fūgērunt.

erat	*was*	patre	*father*
Iovis	*(gen.) of Jupiter*	putāvit	*thought*
ōlim	*once (upon a time)*	igitur	*therefore*
geminōs	*twin*	in (+acc.)	*into*
rēx	*king*	lupam	*wolf*
malus	*wicked*	quae	*who, which*
ā	*from*	nūtrivit	*nursed*

How Rome Got Its Name

Lessons I - XVIII

Agricola ōlim in silvās vēnit et geminōs audīvit. *Ubi* puerōs vīdit, amāvit et *ex* silvīs dūxit. *Post* multōs annōs Rōmulus et Remus erant virī. Urbem *novam* faciēbant, ubi Rōmulus Remum interfēcit. Nōmen "Rōma" ex nōmine "Rōmulō" vēnit. Multī virī vēnērunt et novam urbem *habitābant*. Mūrōs altōs fēcērunt; mūrī *casās* servāvērunt. In casīs *tamen* erant *nullae* fēminae, nullī fīliī, nullae fīliae.

ubi	*when*	habitābant	*lived in*
ex	*out of*	casās	*houses*
post	*after*	tamen	*however*
novam	*new*	nullae	*no, not any*

Lessons I - XX

The founders of Rome were all male. This story tells how the Romans won wives by subterfuge combined with strength.

Rōmānī Sabīnōs virōs, fēminās, filiōs filiāsque ad *lūdōs* vocāvērunt. Ad lūdōs multī Sabīnī vēnērunt; erant nōn īrātī, sed amīcī et piī. Sabīnī *virī* nulla tēla portāvērunt; fēminae filiās et filiōs dūcēbant. *Subitō* Rōmānī filiās Sabīnās cēpērunt et ad *casās* portāvērunt. Parentēs cum filiīs fūgērunt et tēla parāvērunt. *Proximō annō* īrātī virī Sabīnī vēnērunt et pugnāre *parātī* erant. Fīliae tamen Rōmānōs amāvērunt et vocāvērunt: "Estis nōstrī patrēs frātrēsque; sunt virī nostrī. *Nōlite* pugnāre, sed tēla *depōnite.*" *Itaque* Rōmānī et Sabīnī erant amīcī; Sabīnae Rōmānōs Sabīnōsque servāvērunt.

lūdōs	*games*	parātī	*prepared*
virī	*husbands*	nōlite	*don't*
subitō	*suddenly*	depōnite	*put down*
casās	*houses*	itaque	*and so*
proximō annō	*in the next year*		

Fābūla dē Horātiīs et Curiātiīs

Lessons I - XXII

When Rome first began to expand her power, neighboring tribes sought to establish their own supremacy.

Incolae urbis Rōmae in gentīs *aliās* in Italiā pugnābant. Rōmānī deōs invocābant; deī urbem servābant. Albānī ōlim, gēns *finitima*, ad urbem Rōmam vēnērunt et *impetum* in Rōmānōs fēcērunt. Multī Albānī multōs Rōmānōs vulnerāvērunt; multī Rōmānī Albānōs multōs. *Inter* virōs erant *trēs* frātrēs Rōmānī, Horātiī *nōmine*, et trēs frātrēs Albānī, Curiātiī nōmine.

aliās	*other*	inter	*among*
finitima	*neighboring*	trēs	*three*
impetum	*attack*	nōmine	*by name*

Lessons I - XXIV

In extending their power, Romans also extended prosperity. It was in the interest of all to establish victors without killing the vanquished.

Ūnus ex Horātiīs nuntiāvit, "Bellum est malum. Multī erunt vulnerātī; multī erunt *mortuī. Ego* et frātrēs meī pugnābimus cum tribus frātribus Curiātiīs. Trēs frātrēs manēbunt; trēs frātrēs fugient *vel morientur.*" Curiātiī *mox duōs* frātrēs Horātiōs interfēcērunt. Ūnus Horātius sine frātribus, sine amīcīs manēbat. Horātius ab Curiātiīs fugiēbat; Curiātiī post Horātium veniēbant. Ūnus Curiātius erat prō frātribus. Horātius ūnum pugnāvit et interfēcit. Secundus Curiātius ad Horātium vēnit; Horātius secundum interfēcit.

ūnus	*one*	morientur	*they will die*
mortuī	*dead*	mox	*soon*
ego	*I*	duōs	*two*
vel	*or*		

73

Lessons I - XXVI

As the boundaries of Rome's power expanded, Romans overcame many neighboring tribes and assimilated them under Roman rule.

Omnēs frātrēs fuerant audācēs; *ultimī* erant *audācissimī*. Ūnus frāter Horātius cum ūnō Curiātiō pugnāre parābat. Omnēs Rōmānī Albānīque omnēs vidēbant. Curiātius erat ācer sed fessus; Horātius Curiātium interfēcit. Rōmānī erant fēlīcēs. *Rēx* Rōmānōrum factus est rēx Albānōrum quod Horātius Curiātium ultimum interfēcerat. Rōmānum rēgnum erat magnum in Ītaliā.

ultimī	*last*	rēx	*king*
audācissimī	*boldest*		

Fābulae de Ultimō Rēge Rōmānō

Lessons I - XXVIII

The Romans learned to hate tyranny. This story also shows the value put on the chastity of women and the respect paid to honorable suicide.

Rōmulus erat prīmus rēx urbis Rōmae. *Ōmnīnō* erant *septem* rēgēs Rōmae. Ultimus rēx erat Tarquinius Superbus, malus et īrātus. Sextus Tarquinius, fīlius rēgis, *mātrōnam* pulchram Lucrētiam amāvit. Lucrētia Sextum nōn amāvit, sed *frustrā* fūgit. Sextus tamen Lucrētiam cēpit et *dēdecorāvit*. Īrāta et *perturbāta* Lucrētia *sē* interfēcit. Rōmānī *igitur* Sextum Tarquinium et patrem Tarquinium Superbum ex urbe Rōmā mīsērunt. Tarquinius Superbus in proximum regnum fūgit. Rēx Lars Porsenna, amīcus Tarquinōrum, cum exercitū magnō ad urbem Rōmam vēnit et urbem *obsēdit*.

ōmnīnō	*altogether*	perturbāta	*upset*
septem	*seven*	sē	*herself*
mātrōnam	*married lady*	igitur	*therefore*
frustrā	*in vain*	obsēdit	*beseiged*
dēdecorāvit	*dishonored*		

Lessons I - XXX

The valor of one man keeps the enemy out of Rome; the god of the River Tiber saves the man.

Rōmānī omnīs pōntīs trāns flūmen in urbem dēlēbant, sed ūnus pons *nōndum* dēlētus erat. Prīmā lūce exercitus Porsennae ad pontem vēnit. Trēs Rōmānī mīlitēs in ponte stetērunt; nōn mōvērunt, sed pontem tenuērunt. *Post eōs*, amīcī Rōmānī pōntem dēlēbant. *Dēnique* ūnus mīles Rōmānus, Horātius Cōclēs nōmine, in ponte pugnāvit. Amīcī nūntiāvērunt: "Pons dēlētus est! Cāsum pōntis vidēmus!" *Tum* Horātius in flūmen *hīs* verbīs *saluit*: "Pater Tiberīne, accipe *haec* arma et *hunc* mīlitem!" Rōmānī fēlīcēs erant quod Horātius nōn vulnerātus est et urbs servāta est.

nōndum	*not yet*	hīs	*these*
post	*behind*	saluit	*leaped*
eōs	*them*	haec	*these*
dēnique	*finally*	hunc	*this*
tum	*then*		

Lessons I - XXXII

Romans put a high value on courage and loyalty, especially when combined with disdain for physical suffering.

Diū exercitus Porsennae urbem obsidēbat, sed Rōmānī erant audācēs fortēsque et mūrōs tenēbant. Ūnus Rōmānus, Gaius Mūcius nōmine, in *castra* Porsennae nocte vēnit. Rēgem interficere *voluit*, sed Mūcius scrībam *forte* interfēcit. Mūcius vīsus est et captus. Ductus prō rēge, "Rōmānus sum cīvis," inquit, "mē Gaium Mūcium vocant. *Post* mē *alterī* venient. Ūnus *tē* interficiet." Lars Porsenna Mūcium pūnīre voluit. *Tandem* Porsenna Mūcium in *ignem* pōnere *minātus est*. Mūcius *ipse dextram* manum in ignī tenuit. Lars Porsenna Mūcium laudāvit et cīvīs Rōmānōs: "Rōmānī sunt fortēs et nōbilēs; cum Rōmānīs igitur nōn pugnābimus." Exercitum ab urbe Rōmā dūxit. Rōmānī cīvēs erant līberī sub lēgibus sed sine rēge. Mūcius igitur "*Scaevola*" vocātus est quod dextra ignī vulnerāta est.

diū	*for a long time*	tandem	*eventually*
castra	*camp*	ignem	*fire*
voluit	*wanted*	minātus est	*threatened*
forte	*by chance*	ipse	*himself*
post	*after*	dextram	*right (hand)*
alterī	*others*	Scaevola	*Left-handed*
tē	*you*		

Lessons I - XXXIV

After suffering the abuses of monarchy, the Romans chose to share leadership power equally between two men (called consuls) elected annually. In times of crisis, the Senate could appoint a dictator for six months at a time who would have absolute power.

Post septem rēgēs et cāsum Tarquiniī Superbī, Rōmānī cīvēs *rem pūblicam constituērunt*. Duo *consulēs quotannīs* ā cīvibus factī sunt; *libertātem* cīvium et iūra Rōmānōrum servāvērunt. Aeduī ōlim, gēns Gallica, *contrā* Rōmānōs surrēxērunt. Lūcius Quinctius Cincinnātus *cōnsēnsū* omnium dictātor dictus est. Nūntiī ā senātū ad Cincinnātum in agrōs vēnērunt et in urbem vocāvērunt. Cincinnātus pius exercitum Rōmānum contrā Aeduōs dūxit. *Quam celerrimē* Aeduōs *sub iugum* mīsit. *Sextō decimō* diē *dictātūram* dēposuit et cīvis prīvātus īn agrōs revēnit.

rem pūblicam	*republic*	cōnsēnsū	*with the agreement*
constituērunt	*set up*	quam celerrimē	*as quickly as possible*
consulēs	*consuls*	sub iugum	*under the yoke*
quotannīs	*each year*		*(an act of submission)*
libertātem	*freedom*	sextō decimō	*sixteenth*
contrā	*against*	dictātūram	*dictatorship*

Grammatical Catechism for New First Steps

The Sentence

Q: What is a sentence?

A: A sentence is a group of words that contains a subject and a verb and expresses a complete thought.

Q: What are the two parts of a sentence?

A: The two parts of a sentence are the subject and the predicate.

Q: What is the subject of a sentence?

A: The subject of a sentence is the noun or pronoun that the sentence is about.

Q: What is a compound subject?

A: A compound subject consists of more than one noun or pronoun joined by a conjunction.

Q: What is the predicate of a sentence?

A: The predicate is what is said about the subject. It must include a verb.

Q: When does gapping occur?

A: Gapping occurs when the same word is understood in more than one part of a sentence without being repeated.

Parts of Speech

Q: What are the eight parts of speech?

A: The eight parts of speech are: noun, pronoun, adjective, verb, adverb, preposition, conjunction, interjection.

Q: What is a noun?

A: A noun is the name of a person, place, thing, or idea.

Q: What is a pronoun?

A: A pronoun is a word that takes the place of a noun.

Q: What is an adjective?

A: An adjective is a word that modifies a noun or pronoun.

Q: What is a verb?

A: A verb tells what the subject does or has done to it.

Q: What is an adverb?

A: An adverb is a word that modifies a verb, an adjective, or another adverb.

Q: What is a preposition?

A: A preposition is a word that shows the relation of a noun or pronoun to other words in the sentence.

Q: What is a conjunction?

A: A conjunction is a word that connects parts of in a sentence.

Q: What is an interjection?

A: An interjection is an exclamation and does not affect the syntax of the sentence.

Q: What is an article?

A: In English, the words *the*, *a*, and *an* are articles. There are no articles in Latin.

The Noun

Q: How are Latin nouns classified?

A: Latin nouns are classified in five declensions.

Q: How is the 1st Declension marked?

A: The 1st Declension is marked by the ending **-ae** in the genitive singular.

Q: How is the 2nd Declension marked?

A: The 2nd Declension is marked by the ending **-ī** in the genitive singular.

Q: How is the 3rd Declension marked?

A: The 3rd Declension is marked by the ending **-is** in the genitive singular.

Q: How is the 4th Declension marked?

A: The 4th Declension is marked by the ending **-ūs** in the genitive singular.

Q: How is the 5th Declension marked?

A: The 5th Declension is marked by the ending **-eī** in the genitive singular.

Q: What are the uses of a noun in a sentence?

A: The uses of a noun are subject, direct object, indirect object, possessive, object of a preposition, or appositive.

Q: What is an appositive?

A: An appositive is a noun which describes another noun.

Q: What three things do noun endings show?

A: Noun endings show case, number, gender.

Q: What are the five cases of Latin nouns?

A: The five cases of Latin nouns are nominative, genitive, dative, accusative, ablative.

Q: What are the two numbers of Latin nouns?

A: The numbers of Latin nouns are singular and plural.

Q: What are the three genders of Latin nouns?

A: The three genders of Latin nouns are masculine, feminine, neuter.

Q: What are the uses of the nominative case?

A: The uses of the nominative case are subject, predicate nominative, and appositive.

Q: What are the uses of the genitive case?

A: The uses of the genitive case is to show possession.

Q: What are the uses of the dative case?

A: The uses of the dative case are indirect object, with verbs of giving, saying, or showing, and with special adjectives.

Q: What are the uses of the accusative case?

A: The uses of the accusative case are direct object, duration of time, and with prepositions to show motion towards something.

Q: What are the uses of the ablative case?

A: The uses of the ablative case are to express means or time when without a preposition, and with prepositions to show agent, place where, place from which, and accompaniment.

The Verb

Q: What is a transitive verb?

A: A transitive verb may be followed by a direct object.

Q: What is an intransitive verb?

A: An intransitive verb is not followed by a direct object.

Q: What is a linking verb?

A: A linking verb joins the subject with a noun or adjective complement.

Q: What five things does the verb ending show?

A: The verb ending shows person, number, tense, mood, and voice.

Q: What are the persons?

A: The persons are first, second, and third.

Q: What are the numbers?

A: The numbers are singular and plural.

Q: What are the tenses?

A: The tenses are present, imperfect, future, perfect, pluperfect, and future perfect.

Q: What are the moods?

A: The moods are indicative, subjunctive, imperative, infinitive, and participle.

Q: What are the voices?

A: The voices are active and passive.

Q: What does active voice mean?

A: Active voice means the subject is doing something.

Q: What does passive voice mean?

A: Passive voice means something is being done to the subject.

Q: What is the First Rule of Concord?

A: The First Rule of Concord is that a verb must agree in person and number with the subject.

Q: How are Latin verbs classified?

A: Latin verbs are classified in four conjugations.

Q: What marks verbs of the 1st Conjugation?

A: The ending -āre on the second principal part marks verbs of the 1st Conjugation.

Q: What marks verbs of the 2nd Conjugation?

A: The ending -ēre on the second principal part marks verbs of the 2nd Conjugation.

Q: What marks verbs of the 3rd Conjugation?

A: The ending -ere on the second principal part marks verbs of the 3rd Conjugation.

Q: What marks verbs of the 4th Conjugation?

A: The ending -īre on the second principal part marks verbs of the 4th Conjugation.

Q: What is the present system?

A: The present system consists of three tenses that use the present stem.

Q: What three tenses use the present stem?

A: The present, imperfect, and future tenses use the present stem.

Q: What is the perfect system?

A: The perfect system consists of three tenses that use the perfect stems.

Q: What three tenses use the perfect stems?

A: The perfect, pluperfect, and future perfect tenses use the perfect stems.

The Adjective

Q: What three things does the ending of a Latin adjective show?

A: The ending of a Latin adjective shows case, number, and gender.

Q: What is the Second Rule of Concord?

A: The Second Rule of Concord is that an adjective must agree with the noun it modifies in case, number, and gender.

Q: What are the three uses of adjectives?

A: The three uses of adjectives are attributive, predicative, and substantive.

Q: What is the attributive use of an adjective?

A: The attributive use of an adjective modifies a noun without the intervention of a verb.

Q: What is the predicative use of an adjective?

A: The predicative use of an adjective follows a linking verb and completes the meaning of a sentence.

Q: What is the substantive use of an adjective?

A: The substantive use of an adjective replaces the noun in Latin.

Sentence Diagrams

The subject and main verb of a simple sentence are diagrammed onto a single horizontal line. A single vertical line intersecting the horizontal line separates the subject from the predicate.

E.g. Magister laudat.

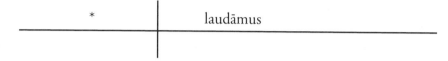

When the subject of the Latin sentence is not expressed by a noun or a pronoun, an asterisk occupies the place of the subject on the main sentence line.

E.g. Laudāmus.

A single vertical line touching the main sentence line separates the direct object from the verb.

E.g. Magister puellam laudat.

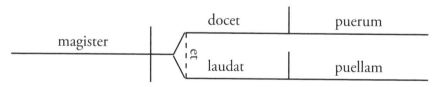

Compound subjects, verbs, and direct objects are diagrammed as follows, with diagonal lines stemming from the main sentence line and leading to parallel lines above and below the main sentence line. The conjunction is written on a vertical dotted line joining the two diagonal lines.

E.g. Magister docet puerum et laudat puellam.

E.g. Puer et puella aquam et silvam laudant.

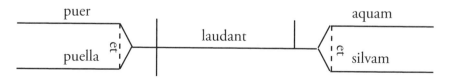

An adjective or an adverb is diagrammed on a diagonal line which touches the main sentence line under the word it modifies.

E.g. Magister bonus puerum nōn laudat.

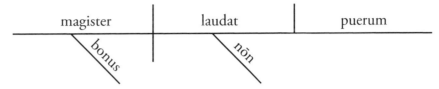

The genitive case is diagrammed on a line parallel to and below the main sentence line, connected to the word it modifies by a diagonal line.

E.g. Fīlius rēgis mūrum mūniet.

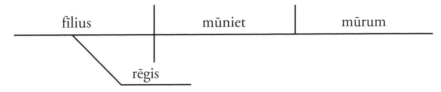

A prepositional phrase is diagrammed like the genitive, but with the preposition on the diagonal line. A prepositional phrase can function either as an adjective or as an adverb.

E.g. Scrība epistulam dē pīrātīs ad ducem portāvit.

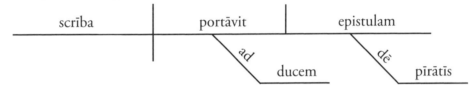

A predicate nominative or adjective is separated from the verb by a diagonal line slanting backwards.

E.g. Mīles erat scrība.

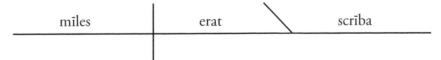

An ablative of means is diagrammed like the genitive.

E.g. Mīles tēlīs vulnerātur.

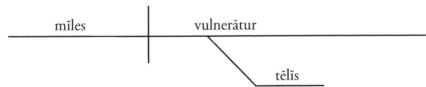

An appositive is placed in parentheses next to the word with which it stands in apposition.

E.g. Mīles, frāter meus, erat scrība.

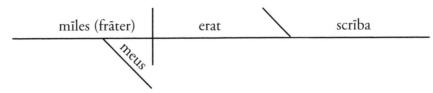

An expression of time is diagrammed like the genitive.

E.g. Mīles multās hōrās pugnābit.

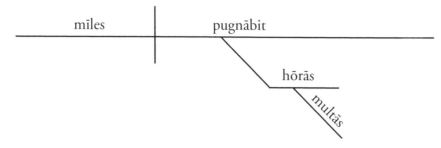

The dative case is diagrammed like the genitive.

E.g. Dux epistulam regī dabit.

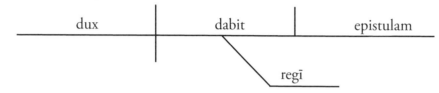

Compound sentences are joined by a dotted line with a step on which the conjunction is written.

E.g. Carmina multa cantābantur et rēgīna laudābātur.

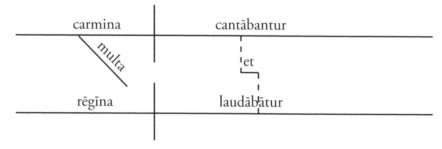

Compound sentences with gapping are diagrammed like regular compound sentences, with the understood word written in parentheses.

E.g. Fīlius epistulam dabit, sed fīlia librum.

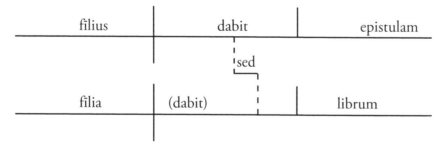

Synopsis of a Verb

AMŌ, AMĀRE, AMĀVĪ, AMĀĀTUM 3ᴿᴰ PERSON PLURAL

Indicative	Active	Passive
Present	ama**nt**	ama**ntur**
Imperfect	amā**bant**	amā**bantur**
Future	amā**bunt**	amā**buntur**
Perfect	amāv**ērunt**	amātī **sunt**
Pluperfect	amāv**erant**	amātī **erant**
Ablative	amāv**erint**	amātī **erunt**

Infinitive	Active	Passive
Present	amā**re**	ama**rī**
Perfect	amā**visse**	amātī **esse**
Future	amāt**ūrus esse**	amāt**um īrī**

Participle	Active	Passive
Present	amā**ns,** amā**ntis**	
Perfect		amāt**us, -a, -um**
Future	amāt**ūrus esse**	amand**um**

Subjunctive	Active	Passive
Present	am**ent**	am**entur**
Imperfect	amā**rent**	amā**rentur**
Perfect	amāv**erint**	amātī **sint**
Pluperfect	amā**vissent**	amātī **essent**

Imperative	Active	Passive
Singular	amā	amā**re**
Plural	amā**te**	amā**minī**

83

Table of the Four Verb Conjugations - Active Voice

Present		First	Second	Third*	Third I-stem*	Fourth
singular	1st	amō	moneō	dūcō	capiō	audiō
	2nd	amās	monēs	dūcis	capis	audīs
	3rd	amat	monet	dūcit	capit	audit
plural	1st	amāmus	monēmus	dūcimus	capimus	audīmus
	2nd	amātis	monētis	dūcitis	capitis	audītis
	3rd	amant	monent	dūcunt	capiunt	audiunt
Imperfect						
singular	1st	amābam	monēbam	dūcēbam	capiēbam	audiēbam
	2nd	amābās	monēbās	dūcēbās	capiēbās	audiēbās
	3rd	amābat	monēbat	dūcēbat	capiēbat	audiēbat
plural	1st	amābāmus	monēbāmus	dūcēbāmus	capiēbāmus	audiēbāmus
	2nd	amābātis	monēbātis	dūcēbātis	capiēbātis	audiēbātis
	3rd	amābant	monēbant	dūcēbant	capiēbant	audiēbant
Future						
singular	1st	amābō	monēbō	dūcam	capiam	audiam
	2nd	amābis	monēbis	dūcēs	capiēs	audiēs
	3rd	amābit	monēbit	dūcet	capiet	audiet
plural	1st	amābimus	monēbimus	dūcēmus	capiēmus	audiēmus
	2nd	amābitis	monēbitis	dūcētis	capiētis	audiētis
	3rd	amābunt	monēbunt	dūcent	capient	audient
Perfect						
singular	1st	amāvī	monuī	dūxī	cēpī	audīvī
	2nd	amāvistī	monuistī	dūxistī	cēpistī	audīvistī
	3rd	amāvit	monuit	dūxit	cēpit	audīvit
plural	1st	amāvimus	monuimus	dūximus	cēpimus	audīvimus
	2nd	amāvistis	monuistis	dūxistis	cēpistis	audīvistis
	3rd	amāvērunt	monuērunt	dūxērunt	cēpērunt	audīvērunt
Pluperfect						
singular	1st	amāveram	monueram	dūxeram	cēperam	audīveram
	2nd	amāverās	monuerās	dūxerās	cēperās	audīverās
	3rd	amāverat	monuerat	dūxerat	cēperat	audīverat
plural	1st	amāverāmus	monuerāmus	dūxerāmus	cēperāmus	audīverāmus
	2nd	amāverātis	monuerātis	dūxerātis	cēperātis	audīverātis
	3rd	amāverant	monuerant	dūxerant	cēperant	audīverant
Future Perfect						
singular	1st	amāverō	monuerō	dūxerō	cēperō	audīverō
	2nd	amāveris	monueris	dūxeris	cēperis	audīveris
	3rd	amāverit	monuerit	dūxerit	cēperit	audīverit
plural	1st	amāverimus	monuerimus	dūxerimus	cēperimus	audīverimus
	2nd	amāveritis	monueritis	dūxeritis	cēperitis	audīveritis
	3rd	amāverint	monuerint	dūxerint	cēperint	audīverint

*Third Conjugation has a variable vowel.

Table of the Four Verb Conjugations - Passive Voice

Present		First	Second	Third*	Third I-stem*	Fourth
singular	1st	amor	moneor	dūcor	capior	audior
	2nd	amāris	monēris	dūceris	caperis	audīris
	3rd	amātur	monētur	dūcitur	capitur	audītur
plural	1st	amāmur	monēmur	dūcimur	capimur	audīmur
	2nd	amāminī	monēminī	dūciminī	capiminī	audīminī
	3rd	amantur	monentur	dūcuntur	capiuntur	audiuntur

Imperfect						
singular	1st	amābar	monēbar	dūcēbar	capiēbar	audiēbar
	2nd	amābāris	monēbāris	dūcēbāris	capiēbāris	audiēbāris
	3rd	amābātur	monēbātur	dūcēbātur	capiēbātur	audiēbātur
plural	1st	amābāmur	monēbāmur	dūcēbāmur	capiēbāmur	audiēbāmur
	2nd	amābāminī	monēbāminī	dūcēbāminī	capiēbāminī	audiēbāminī
	3rd	amābantur	monēbantur	dūcēbantur	capiēbantur	audiēbantur

Future						
singular	1st	amābor	monēbor	dūcar	capiar	audiar
	2nd	amāberis	monēberis	dūcēris	capiēris	audiēris
	3rd	amābitur	monēbitur	dūcētur	capiētur	audiētur
plural	1st	amābimur	monēbimur	dūcēmur	capiēmur	audiēmur
	2nd	amābiminī	monēbiminī	dūcēminī	capiēminī	audiēminī
	3rd	amābuntur	monēbuntur	dūcentur	capientur	audientur

Perfect						
singular	1st	amātus/a sum	monitus/a sum	ductus/a sum	captus/a sum	audītus/a sum
	2nd	amātus/a es	monitus/a es	ductus/a es	captus/a es	audītus/a es
	3rd	amātus/a/um est	monitus/a/um est	ductus/a/um est	captus/a/um est	audītus/a/um est
plural	1st	amātī/ae sumus	monitī/ae sumus	ductī/ae sumus	captī/ae sumus	audītī/ae sumus
	2nd	amātī/ae estis	monitī/ae estis	ductī/ae estis	captī/ae estis	audītī/ae estis
	3rd	amātī/ae/a sunt	monitī/ae/a sunt	ductī/ae/a sunt	captī/ae/a sunt	audītī/ae/a sunt

Pluperfect						
singular	1st	amātus/a eram	monitus/a eram	ductus/a eram	captus/a eram	audītus/a eram
	2nd	amātus/a erās	monitus/a erās	ductus/a erās	captus/a erās	audītus/a erās
	3rd	amātus/a/um erat	monitus/a/um erat	ductus/a/um erat	captus/a/um erat	audītus/a/um erat
plural	1st	amātī/ae erāmus	monitī/ae erāmus	ductī/ae erāmus	captī/ae erāmus	audītī/ae erāmus
	2nd	amātī/ae erātis	monitī/ae erātis	ductī/ae erātis	captī/ae erātis	audītī/ae erātis
	3rd	amātī/ae/a erant	monitī/ae/a erant	ductī/ae/a erant	captī/ae/a erant	audītī/ae/a erant

Future Perfect						
singular	1st	amātus/a erō	monitus/a erō	ductus/a erō	captus/a erō	audītus/a erō
	2nd	amātus/a eris	monitus/a eris	ductus/a eris	captus/a eris	audītus/a eris
	3rd	amātus/a/um erit	monitus/a/um erit	ductus/a/um erit	captus/a/um erit	audītus/a/um erit
plural	1st	amātī/ae erimus	monitī/ae erimus	ductī/ae erimus	captī/ae erimus	audītī/ae erimus
	2nd	amātī/ae eritis	monitī/ae eritis	ductī/ae eritis	captī/ae eritis	audītī/ae eritis
	3rd	amātī/ae/a erunt	monitī/ae/a erunt	ductī/ae/a erunt	captī/ae/a erunt	audītī/ae/a erunt

*Third Conjugation has a variable vowel.

Table of the Five Noun Declensions

Singular	First M/F	Second M	N	Third M/F	N	Fourth M/F	N	Fifth M/F
Nominative	puella	dominus	verbum	mīles	opus	gradus	cornū	rēs
Genitive	puellae	dominī	verbī	mīlitis	operis	gradūs	cornūs	reī
Dative	puellae	dominō	verbō	mīlitī	operī	graduī	cornū	reī
Accusative	puellam	dominum	verbum	mīlitem	opus	gradum	cornū	rem
Ablative	puellā	dominō	verbō	mīlite	opere	gradū	cornū	rē
Plural								
Nominative	puellae	dominī	verba	mīlitēs	opera	gradūs	cornua	rēs
Genitive	puellārum	dominōrum	verbōrum	mīlitum	operum	graduum	cornuum	rērum
Dative	puellīs	dominīs	verbīs	mīlitibus	operibus	gradibus	cornibus	rēbus
Accusative	puellās	dominōs	verba	mīlitēs	opera	gradūs	cornua	rēs
Ablative	puellīs	dominīs	verbīs	mīlitibus	operibus	gradibus	cornibus	rēbus

Table of Adjectives – First And Second Declension

	Singular			Plural		
	M	F	N	M	F	N
Nominative	bon**us**	bon**a**	bon**um**	bon**ī**	bon**ae**	bon**a**
Genitive	bon**ī**	bon**ae**	bon**ī**	bon**ōrum**	bon**ārum**	bon**ōrum**
Dative	bon**ō**	bon**ae**	bon**ō**	bon**īs**	bon**īs**	bon**īs**
Accusative	bon**um**	bon**am**	bon**um**	bon**ōs**	bon**ās**	bon**a**
Ablative	bon**ō**	bon**ā**	bon**ō**	bon**īs**	bon**īs**	bon**īs**

	Singular			Plural		
	M	F	N	M	F	N
Nominative	sacer	sacr**a**	sacr**um**	sacr**ī**	sacr**ae**	sacr**a**
Genitive	sacr**ī**	sacr**ae**	sacr**ī**	sacr**ōrum**	sacr**ārum**	sacr**ōrum**
Dative	sacr**ō**	sacr**ae**	sacr**ō**	sacr**īs**	sacr**īs**	sacr**īs**
Accusative	sacr**um**	sacr**am**	sacr**um**	sacr**ōs**	sacr**ās**	sacr**a**
Ablative	sacr**ō**	sacr**ā**	sacr**ō**	sacr**īs**	sacr**īs**	sacr**īs**

	Singular			Plural		
	M	F	N	M	F	N
Nominative	miser	miser**a**	miser**um**	miser**ī**	miser**ae**	miser**a**
Genitive	miser**ī**	miser**ae**	miser**ī**	miser**ōrum**	miser**ārum**	miser**ōrum**
Dative	miser**ō**	miser**ae**	miser**ō**	miser**īs**	miser**īs**	miser**īs**
Accusative	miser**um**	miser**am**	miser**um**	miser**ōs**	miser**ās**	miser**a**
Ablative	miser**ō**	miser**ā**	miser**ō**	miser**īs**	miser**īs**	miser**īs**

Table of Adjectives - Third Declension

Three Terminations						
	Singular			Plural		
	M	F	N	M	F	N
Nominative	ācer	ācr**is**	ācr**e**	ācr**ēs**	ācr**ēs**	ācr**ia**
Genitive	ācr**is**	ācr**is**	ācr**is**	ācr**ium**	ācr**ium**	ācr**ium**
Dative	ācr**ī**	ācr**ī**	ācr**ī**	ācr**ibus**	ācr**ibus**	ācr**ibus**
Accusative	ācr**em**	ācr**em**	ācr**e**	ācr**īs/ēs**	ācr**īs/ēs**	ācr**ia**
Ablative	ācr**ī**	ācr**ī**	ācr**ī**	ācr**ibus**	ācr**ibus**	ācr**ibus**

Two Terminations					**One Termination**			
	Singular		Plural			Singular		Plural	
	M/F	N	M/F	N		M/F	N	M/F	N
Nominative	omn**is**	omn**e**	omn**es**	omn**ia**	Nominative	fēlīx	fēlīx	fēlīc**ēs**	fēlīc**ia**
Genitive	omn**is**	omn**is**	omn**ium**	omn**ium**	Genitive	fēlīc**is**	fēlīc**is**	fēlīc**ium**	fēlīc**ium**
Dative	omn**ī**	omn**ī**	omn**ibus**	omn**ibus**	Dative	fēlīc**ī**	fēlīc**ī**	fēlīc**ibus**	fēlīc**ibus**
Accusative	omn**em**	omn**e**	omn**īs/ēs**	omn**ia**	Accusative	fēlīc**em**	fēlīx	fēlīc**īs/ēs**	fēlīc**ia**
Ablative	omn**ī**	omn**ī**	omn**ibus**	omn**ibus**	Ablative	fēlīc**ī**	fēlīc**ī**	fēlīc**ibus**	fēlīc**ibus**

Classified Vocabulary

Verbs

1st Conjugation

amō, amāre, amāvī, amātum, *love, like*
cantō, cantāre, cantāvī, cantātum, *sing*
errō, errāre, errāvī, errātum, *wander, make a mistake*
laudō, laudāre, laudāvī, laudātum, *praise*
monstrō, monstrāre, monstrāvī, monstrātum, *show*
nuntiō, nuntiāre, nuntiāvī, nuntiātum, *report, announce*
parō, parāre, parāvī, parātum, *prepare*
portō, portāre, portāvī, portātum, *carry*
pugnō, pugnāre, pugnāvī, pugnātum, *fight*
rogō, rogāre, rogāvī, rogātum, *ask*
servō, servāre, servāvī, servātum, *watch over, guard, save*
stō, stāre, stetī, stātum, *stand*
vocō, vocāre, vocāvī, vocātum, *call*
vulnerō, vulnerāre, vulnerāvī, vulnerātum, *wound, hurt*

2nd Conjugation

dēleō, dēlēre, dēlēvī, dēlētum, *destroy*
doceō, docēre, docuī, doctum, *teach*
maneō, manēre, mānsī, mānsum, *remain, stay*
moneō, monēre, monuī, monitum, *warn, advise*
moveō, movēre, mōvī, mōtum, *move*
sedeō, sedēre, sēdī, sessum, *sit*
teneō, tenēre, tenuī, tentum, *hold, contain*
terreō, terrēre, terruī, territum, *frighten*
timeō, timēre, timuī, —, *fear, be afraid of*
videō, vidēre, vīdī, vīsum, *see*

3rd Conjugation

cernō, cernere, crēvī, crētum, *perceive, discern; decide*
dīcō, dīcere, dīxī, dictum, *say, speak, tell*
dūcō, dūcere, dūxī, ductum, *lead*
gerō, gerere, gessī, gestum, *carry on*
mittō, mittere, mīsī, missum, *send*
pōnō, pōnere, posuī, positum, *put, place, set up*
regō, regere, rēxī, rēctum, *rule*
scrībō, scrībere, scripsī, scriptum, *write*
surgō, surgere, surrēxī, surrēctum, *rise, swell, stretch upward*
tegō, tegere, tēxī, tēctum, *cover, conceal, shelter*
tendō, tendere, tetendī, tensum/tentum, *extend, stretch out, proceed*
volvō, volvere, volvī, volūtum, *roll*

3rd Conjugation -iō

accipiō, accipere, accēpī, acceptum, *receive*
capiō, capere, cēpī, captum, *take, seize, capture*
faciō, facere, fēcī, factum, *make, do*
fugiō, fugere, fūgī, fugitum, *flee, run away, avoid*
interficiō, -ficere, -fēcī, -fectum, *kill*

4th Conjugation

audiō, audīre, audīvī, audītum, *hear, listen to*
mūniō, mūnīre, mūnīvī, mūnītum, *fortify, build*
pūniō, pūnīre, pūnīvī, pūnītum, *punish*
veniō, venīre, vēnī, ventum, *come*

Irregular

dō, dare, dedī, datum, *give*
sum, esse, fuī, futūrus, *be*

Nouns

1st Declension: Feminine

aqua, -ae, f., *water*
dea, -ae, f., *goddess*
epistula, -ae, f., *letter*
fīlia, -ae, f., *daughter*
hōra, -ae, f., *hour*
īra, -ae, f., *anger, wrath*
ōra, -ae, f., *shore, rim, edge*
patria, -ae, f., *native land*
porta, -ae, f., *gate*
puella, -ae, f., *girl*
rēgīna, -ae, f., *queen*
silva, -ae, f., *forest, woods*
terra, -ae, f., *land, earth, a country*
umbra, -ae, f., *shadow, ghost*

1st Declension: Masculine

agricola, -ae, m., *farmer*
incola, -ae m., *inhabitant*
nauta, -ae, m., *sailor*
pīrāta, -ae, m., *pirate*
poēta, -ae, m., *poet*
scrība, -ae, m., *writer, secretary*

2nd Declension: Masculine

ager, agrī, m., *field*
annus, -ī, m., *year*
campus, -ī, m., *plain, field, playing field*
deus, -ī, m., *god*
dominus, -ī, m., *master*
fīlius, -ī, m., *son*
liber, librī, m., *book*
magister, magistrī, m., *teacher*
mūrus, -ī, m., *wall*
nuntius, -ī, m., *messenger*
puer, puerī, m., *boy*
servus, -ī, m., *slave*
somnus, -ī, m., *sleep*
ventus, ī, m., *wind*
vir, virī, m., *man*

2nd Declension: Neuter

bellum, -ī, n., *war*
dōnum, -ī, n., *gift*
factum, -ī, n., *deed*
rēgnum, -ī, n., *kingdom*
tēlum, -ī, n., *weapon, javelin*
verbum, -ī, n., *word*

3rd Declension: Masculine

cīvis, cīvis, m.+ f., (-ium) *citizen*
dux, ducis, m., *leader*
frāter, frātris, m., *brother*
mīles, mīlitis, m., *soldier*
mons, montis, m., (-ium) *mountain*
pater, patris, m., *father*
pons, pontis, m., (-ium) *bridge*
rex, rēgis, m., *king*

3rd Declension: Feminine

cīvis, cīvis, m.+ f., (-ium) *citizen*
gens, gentis, f., (-ium) *tribe, nation*
lex, lēgis, f., *law*
lux, lūcis, f., *light*
māter, mātris, f., *mother*
nāvis, nāvis, f., (-ium) *ship*
nox, noctis, f., (-ium) *night*
soror, sorōris, f., *sister*
urbs, urbis, f., (-ium) *city*
vox, vōcis, f., *voice*

3rd Declension: Neuter

caput, capitis, n., *head*
carmen, carminis, n., *song*
corpus, corporis, n., *body*
flūmen, flūminis, n. *river*
iter, itineris, n., *journey, road, way*
iūs, iūris, n., *right, law*
lītus, lītoris, n., *shore, coast, beach*
mare, maris, n., (-ium) *sea*
nōmen, nōminis, n., *name*
onus, oneris, n., *burden*
opus, operis, n., *work, task*
pectus, pectoris, n., *breast, chest, heart*

4th Declension: Masculine

cāsus, -ūs, m., *chance, misfortune; fall*
exercitus, -ūs, m., *army*
fluctus, -ūs, m., *wave, flood; (pl.) sea*
gradus, -ūs, m., *step*

4th Declension: Feminine

domus, -ūs, f., *home, household*
manus, -ūs, f., *hand*

4th Declension: Neuter

cornū, -ūs, n., *horn*

5th Declension

diēs, -ēī, m., *day*
fidēs, -eī, f., *faith, loyalty*
rēs, -eī, f., *thing, affair, matter*
speciēs, -ēī, f., *appearance, sight*
spēs, speī, f., *hope*

Adjectives

1st and 2nd Declension: 3 terminations

aeger, aegra, aegrum, *sick*
āter, ātra, ātrum, *dark, black*
altus, -a, -um, *high, deep, tall*
amīcus, -a, -um, *friendly*
bonus, -a, -um, *good*
cārus, -a, -um, *dear*
fessus, -a, -um, *tired, exhausted*
īrātus, -a, -um, *angry*
miser, misera, miserum, *unhappy, wretched*
līber, lībera, līberum, *free*
longus, -a, -um, *long*
magnus, -a, -um, *great, large*
malus, -a, -um, *evil, bad, wicked*
meus, -a, -um, *my, mine*
multus, -a, -um, *much; (pl.) many*
noster, nostra, nostrum, *our*
parvus, -a, -um, *small, little*
pius, -a, -um, *dutiful, devoted, loyal*
prīmus, -a, -um, *first*
proximus, -a, -um, *next*
pulcher, pulchra, pulchrum, *beautiful*
sacer, sacra, sacrum, *holy*
tuus, -a, -um, *your, yours* (belonging to one person)
vester, vestra, vestrum, *your, yours* (belonging to more than
    one person)

3rd Declension: 3 terminations

ācer, ācris, ācre, *sharp, fierce, keen*
celer, celeris, celere, *swift, quick*

3rd Declension: 2 terminations

brevis, -e, *short, brief*
difficilis, -e, *difficult*
dulcis, -e, *sweet*
facilis, -e, *easy*
fortis, -e, *brave, strong*
gravis, -e, *heavy, serious*
similis, -e, *similar, like*
omnis, -e, *every, all*
tristis, -e, *sad*
ūtilis, -e, *useful*

3rd Declension: 1 termination

audāx, audācis, *bold*
fēlīx, fēlīcis, *happy*
īngēns, ingentis, *huge, vast*
sapiēns, sapientis, *wise*

Prepositions

ā, ab, (+ abl.) *by; from, away from*
ad, *to, towards, at*
cum, (+ abl.) *with, along with*
dē, (+ abl.) *about, concerning; down from*
ē, ex, (+ abl.) *from, out of*
in, (+ acc.) *into, onto, against*; (+ abl.) *in, on*
prō, (+ abl.) *in front of; on behalf of*
sine, (+ abl.) *without*
sub, (+ abl.) *under*

Conjunctions

et, *and*
-que, *and*
quod, *because*
sed, *but*

Adverb

nōn, *not*

Vocabulary

Nouns: The nominative singular of each noun is given followed by the genitive singular. For regular first, second, fourth and fifth declension nouns, only the genitive singular ending is given (e.g. **mūrus, -ī**). Where the stem cannot be determined from the nominative singular form, as in some second declension nouns and in the third declension, the full form of the genitive singular is given.

Adjectives: Adjectives have the nominative singular forms for all genders given. For regular first and second declension adjectives, and for regular third declension adjectives of two terminations, only the endings of the feminine and neuter are given (e.g. **bonus, -a, -um**). Where the stem cannot be determined from the nominative singular masculine form, the full forms are given. In the case of third declension adjectives of one termination, the nominative singular form is followed by the genitive singular form.

Verbs: The first person singular present indicative active of each verb is listed. If the verb is regular (i.e. forms its stems like **amō, moneō,** or **audiō**), a numeral follows to indicate its conjugation (**laudō** (1), *I praise*). If the verb is irregular, its principal parts follow.

At the end of each entry, the chapter number in which the word was introduced is given in square brackets.

LATIN – ENGLISH VOCABULARY

A

ā, ab, (+ abl.) *by* [XXII]; *from, away from* [XXIV]
accipiō, accipere, accēpī, acceptum, *receive* [XVII]
ācer, ācris, ācre, *sharp, fierce, keen* [XXV]
ad, (+ acc.) *to, towards, at* [XVII]
aeger, aegra, aegrum, *sick* [XVII]
ager, agrī, m., *field* [VIII]
agricola, -ae, m., *farmer* [IV]
altus, -a, -um, *high, deep, tall* [XII]
amīcus, -a, -um, *friendly* [XVIII]
amīcus, amīcī, m., *friend* [XVIII]
amō (1), *love, like* [I]
annus, -ī, m., *year* [XXVIII]
aqua, -ae, f., *water* [V]
āter, ātra, ātrum, *dark, black* [XVII]
audax, audācis, *bold* [XXVI]
audiō (4), *hear, listen to* [XIV]

B

bellum, -ī, n., *war* [XV]
bonus, -a, -um, *good* [XII]
brevis, -e, *short, brief* [XXVI]

C

campus, -ī, m., *plain, field, playing field* [XV]
cantō (1), *sing* [II]
capiō, capere, cēpī, captum, *take, seize, capture* [XVI]
caput, capitis, n., *head* [XXIII]
cārus, -a, -um, *dear* [XXXI]
cāsus, -ūs, m., *chance, misfortune; fall* [XXIX]
carmen, carminis, n., *song* [XX]
celer, celeris, celere, *swift, quick* [XXV]
cernō, cernere, crēvī, crētum, *perceive, discern; decide* [XXX]

cīvis, cīvis, m. and f., *citizen* [XXI]
cornū, -ūs, n., *horn* [XXIX]
corpus, corporis, n., *body* [XXIII]
cum, (+ abl.) *with, along with* [XXIV]

D

dē, (+ abl.) *about, concerning; down from* [XXIV]
dea, -ae, f., *goddess* [XI]
dēleō, dēlēre, dēlēvī, dēlētum, *destroy* [XXVII]
deus, -ī, m., *god* [VIII]
dīcō, dīcere, dīxī, dictum, *say, speak, tell* [XXVIII]
diēs, -ēī, m., *day* [XXXII]
difficilis, -e, *difficult* [XXXII]
dō, dare, dedī, datum, *give* [XXXI]
doceō, docēre, docuī, doctum, *teach* [VI]
dominus, -ī, m., *master* [VIII]
domus, -ūs, f., *home, household* [XXIX]
dōnum, -ī, n., *gift* [XXXI]
dūcō, dūcere, duxī, ductum, *lead* [X]
dulcis, -e, *sweet* [XXX]
dux, ducis, m., *leader* [XIX]

E

ē, ex, (+ abl.) *from, out of* [XXIV]
epistula, -ae, f., *letter* [V]
errō (1), *wander, make a mistake* [II]
et, *and* [III]
exercitus, -ūs, m., *army* [XXIX]

F

facilis, -e, *easy* [XXXII]
faciō, facere, fēcī, factum, *make, do* [XVI]
    (iter facere, *to make a journey, to march*) [XVI]
factum, -ī, n., *deed* [IX]

91

fēlīx, fēlīcis, *happy* [XXVI]
fessus, -a, -um, *tired, exhausted* [XVIII]
fidēs, -eī, f., *faith, loyalty* [XXXII]
fīlia, -ae, f., *daughter* [XI]
fīlius, -ī, m., *son* [XI]
fluctus, -ūs, m., *wave, flood; (pl.) sea* [XXIX]
flūmen, flūminis, n. *river* [XX]
fortis, -e, *brave, strong* [XXIX]
frāter, frātris, m., *brother* [XXVI]
fugiō, fugere, fūgī, fugitum, *flee, run away, avoid* [XVI]

G

gēns, gentis, f., *tribe, nation* [XXI]
gerō, gerere, gessī, gestum, *carry on* (bellum gerere, *to wage war*) [XXX]
gradus, -ūs, m., *step* [XXIX]
gravis, -e, *heavy, serious* [XXX]

H

hōra, -ae, f., *hour* [XXVIII]

I

in, (+ acc.) *into, onto, against* [XVII]; (+ abl.) *in, on* [XXIV]
incola, -ae m., *inhabitant* [XXII]
ingēns, ingentis, *huge, vast* [XXXIII]
interficiō, -ficere, -fēcī, -fectum, *kill* [XVII]
īra, -ae, f., *anger, wrath* [VII]
īrātus, -a, -um, *angry* [XVIII]
iter, itineris, n., *journey, road, way* [XXIII]
iūs, iūris, n., *right, law* [XXIII]

L

laudō (1), *praise* [I]
lex, lēgis, f., *law* [XIX]
līber, lībera, līberum, *free* [XIII]
liber, librī, m., *book* [VIII]
lītus, lītoris, n., *shore, coast, beach* [XX]
longus, -a, -um, *long* [XX]
lux, lūcis, f., *light* [XXV]

M

magister, magistrī, m., *teacher* [VIII]
magnus, -a, -um, *great, large* [XII]
malus, -a, -um, *evil, bad, wicked* [XVIII]
maneō, manēre, mānsī, mānsum, *remain, stay* [XXIV]
manus, -ūs, f., *hand* [XXIX]
mare, maris, n., *sea* [XXI]
māter, mātris, f., *mother* [XXVI]
meus, -a, -um, *my, mine* [XII]
mīles, mīlitis, m., *soldier* [XIX]
miser, misera, miserum, *unhappy, wretched* [XIII]
mittō, mittere, mīsī, missum, *send* [X]
moneō (2), *warn, advise* [VI]
mons, montis, m., *mountain* [XXV]
monstrō (1), *show* [XXII]
moveō, movēre, mōvī, mōtum, *move* [XXVII]
multus, -a, -um, *much; (pl.) many* [XII]

mūniō (4), *fortify, build* [XIV]
mūrus, -ī, m., *wall* [XV]

N

nauta, -ae, m., *sailor* [XXII]
nāvis, nāvis, f., *ship* [XXI]
nōmen, nōminis, n., *name* [XX]
nōn, *not* [I]
noster, nostra, nostrum, *our* [XIII]
nox, noctis, f., *night* [XXV]
nūntiō (1), *report, announce* [XXII]
nūntius, -ī, m., *messenger* [XI]

O

omnis, -e, *every, all* [XXVI]
onus, oneris, n., *burden* [XX]
opus, operis, n., *work, task* [XX]
ōra, -ae, f., *shore, rim, edge* [XVI]

P

parō (1), *prepare* [III]
parvus, -a, -um, *small, little* [XII]
pater, patris, m., *father* [XXVI]
patria, -ae, f., *native land* [V]
pectus, pectoris, n., *breast, chest, heart* [XXIII]
pīrāta, -ae, m., *pirate* [XXII]
pius, -a, -um, *dutiful, devoted, loyal* [XVIII]
poēta, -ae, m., *poet* [IV]
pōnō, pōnere, posuī, positum, *put, place, set up* [X]
pons, pontis, m., *bridge* [XXV]
porta, -ae, f., *gate* [VII]
portō (1), *carry* [II]
prīma lūx, prīmae lūcis, f., *dawn* [XXVIII}
prīmus, -a, -um, *first* [XXVIII]
prō, (+ abl.) *in front of; on behalf of* [XXIV]
proximus, -a, -um, *next* [XXVIII]
puella, -ae, f., *girl* [IV]
puer, puerī, m., *boy* [IX]
pugnō (1), *fight* [II]
pulcher, pulchra, pulchrum, *beautiful* [XIII]
pūniō (4), *punish* [XIV]

Q

-que, *and* [XIV]
quod, *because* [XIV]

R

rēgīna, -ae, f., *queen* [IV]
regnum, -ī, n., *kingdom* [XXV]
regō, regere, rēxī, rēctum, *rule* [XXVIII]
rēs, -eī, f., *thing, affair, matter* [XXXII]
rex, rēgis, m., *king* [XXVII]
rogō (1), *ask* [I]

S

sacer, sacra, sacrum, *holy* [XIII]
sapiēns, sapientis, *wise* [XXXIII]

92

scrība, -ae, m., *writer, secretary* [XXII]

scrībō, scrībere, scrīpsī, scrīptum, *write* [X]

sed, *but*

sedeō, sedēre, sēdī, sessum, *sit* [XXIV]

servō (1), *watch over, guard, save* [III]

servus, -ī, m., *slave* [XV]

silva, -ae, f., *forest, woods* [VII]

similis, -e, *similar, like* [XXXI]

sine, (+ abl.) *without* [XXIV]

somnus, -ī, m., *sleep* [XV]

soror, sorōris, f., *sister* [XIX]

speciēs, -ēī, f., *appearance, sight* [XXXII]

spēs, speī, f., *hope* [XXXII]

stō, stāre, stetī, stātum, *stand* [XXIV]

sub, (+ abl.) *under* [XXIV]

sum, esse, fuī, futūrus, *be* [XVIII]

surgō, surgere, surrexī, surrectum, *rise, swell, stretch upward* [XXXIII]

T

tegō, tegere, texī, tectum, *cover, conceal, shelter* [XXX]

tēlum, -ī, n., *weapon, javelin* [XV]

tendō, tendere, tetendī, tensum/tentum, *extend, stretch out, proceed* [XXXIII]

teneō, tenēre, tenuī, tentum, *hold, contain* [VI]

terra, -ae, f., *land, earth, a country* [XVI]

terreō (2), *frighten* [VI]

timeō, timēre, timuī, -, *fear, be afraid of* [IX]

tristis, -e, *sad* [XXXIII]

tuus, -a, -um, *your, yours* (belonging to one person) [XII]

U

umbra, -ae, f., *shadow, ghost* [VII]

urbs, urbis, f., *city* [XXI]

ūtilis, -e, *useful* [XXXI]

V

veniō, venīre, vēnī, ventum, *come* [XIV]

ventus, ī, m., *wind* [XV]

verbum, -ī, n., *word* [IX]

vester, vestra, vestrum, *your, yours* (belonging to more than one person) [XIII]

videō, vidēre, vīdī, vīsum, *see* [VII]

vir, virī, m., *man* [IX]

vocō (1), *call* [I]

volvō, volvere, volvī, volūtum, *roll* [XXX]

vox, vōcis, f., *voice* [XIX]

vulnerō (1), *wound, hurt* [I]

ENGLISH – LATIN VOCABULARY

A

about, dē, (+ abl.) [XXIV]

advise, moneō (2) [VI]

affair, rēs, -eī, f. [XXXII]

against, in, (+ acc.) [XVII]

all, omnis, omne [XXVI]

along with, cum, (+ abl.) [XXIV]

and, et [III], -que [XIV]

anger, īra, -ae, f. [VII]

angry, īrātus, -a, -um [XVIII]

announce, nūntiō (1) [XXII]

appearance, speciēs, -ēī, f. [XXXII]

army, exercitus, -ūs, m. [XXIX]

ask, rogō (1) [I]

at, ad [XVII]

avoid, fugiō, fugere, fūgī, fugitum [XVI]

away from, ā, ab, (+ abl.) [XXIV]

B

bad, malus, -a, -um [XVIII]

be, sum, esse, fuī, futūrus [XVIII]

be afraid of, timeō, timēre, timuī, - [IX]

beach, lītus, lītoris, n. [XX]

beautiful, pulcher, pulchra, pulchrum [XIII]

because, quod [XIV]

before, prō (+abb.) [XXIV]

black, āter, ātra, ātrum [XVII]

body, corpus, corporis, n. [XXIII]

bold, audax, audācis [XXVI]

book, liber, librī, m. [VIII]

boy, puer, puerī, m. [IX]

brave, fortis, -e [XXIX]

breast, pectus, pectoris, n. [XXIII]

bridge, pons, pontis, m. [XXV]

brief, brevis, -e [XXVI]

brother, frāter, frātris, m. [XXVI]

build, mūniō (4) [XIV]

burden, onus, oneris, n. [XX]

but, sed

by, ā, ab, (+ abl.) [XXII]

C

call, vocō (1) [I]

capture, capiō, capere, cēpī, captum [XVI]

carry on, gerō, gerere, gessī, gestum [XXX]

carry, portō (1) [II]

chance, cāsus, -ūs, m. [XXIX]

chest, pectus, pectoris, n. [XXIII]

citizen, cīvis, cīvis, m. and f. [XXI]

city, urbs, urbis, f. [XXI]

coast, lītus, lītoris, n. [XX]

come, veniō, venīre, vēnī, ventum [XIV]

conceal, tegō, tegere, texī, tectum [XXX]

concerning, dē, (+ abl.) [XXIV]

contain, teneō, tenēre, tenuī, tentum, [VI]

country, terra, -ae, f. [XVI]
cover, tegō, tegere, tēxī, tēctum [XXX]

D

dark, āter, ātra, ātrum [XVII]
daughter, fīlia, -ae, f. [XI]
dawn, prīma lūx, prīmae lūcis, f. [XXVIII]
day, diēs, -ēī, m. [XXXII]
dear, cārus, -a, -um [XXXI]
deed, factum, -ī, n. [IX]
deep, altus, -a, -um [XII]
destroy, dēleō, dēlēre, dēlēvī, dēlētum [XXVII]
devoted, pius, -a, -um [XVIII]
difficult, difficilis, -e [XXXII]
discern, cernō, cernere, crēvī, crētum [XXX]
do, faciō, facere, fēcī, factum [XVI]
down from, dē, (+ abl.) [XXIV]
dutiful, pius, -a, -um [XVIII]

E

earth, terra, -ae, f. [XVI]
easy, facilis, -e [XXXII]
edge, ōra, -ae, f. [XVI]
every, omnis, omne [XXVI]
evil, malus, -a, -um [XVIII]
exhausted, fessus, -a, -um [XVIII]
extend, tendō, tendere, tetendī, tensum/tentum [XXXIII]

F

faith, fidēs, -eī f. [XXXII]
fall, cāsus, -ūs, m. [XXIX]
farmer agricola, -ae, m. [IV]
father, pater, patris, m. [XXVI]
fear, timeō, timēre, timuī, - [IX]
field, ager, agrī, m.[VIII]; *playing field,* campus, -ī, m. [XV]
fierce, ācer, ācris, ācre [XXV]
fight, pugnō (1) [II]
first, prīmus, -a, -um [XXVIII]
flee, fugiō, fugere, fūgī, fugitum [XVI]
flood, fluctus, -ūs, m. [XXIX]
forest, silva, -ae, f. [VII]
fortify, mūniō (4) [XIV]
free, līber, lībera, līberum [XIII]
friend, amīcus, -ī, [XVIII]
friendly, amīcus, -a, -um [XVIII]
frighten, terreō (2) [VI]
from, ā, ab, (+ abl.) [XXIV], ē, ex, (+ abl.) [XXIV]

G

gate, porta, -ae, f. [VII]
ghost, umbra, -ae, f. [VII]
gift, dōnum, -ī, n. [XXXI]
girl, puella, -ae, f. [IV]
give, dō, dare, dedī, datum [XXXI]
god, deus, -ī, m. [VIII]
goddess, dea, -ae, f. [XI]
good, bonus, -a, -um [XII]

great, magnus, -a, -um [XII]

H

hand, manus, -ūs, f. [XXIX]
happy, fēlīx, fēlīcis [XXVI]
head, caput, capitis, n. [XXIII]
hear, audiō (4) [XIV]
heart, pectus, pectoris, n. [XXIII]
heavy, gravis, -e [XXX]
high, altus, -a, -um [XII]
hold, teneō, tenēre, tenuī, tentum [VI]
holy, sacer, sacra, sacrum [XIII]
home, domus, -ūs, f. [XXIX]
hope, spēs, speī, f. [XXXII]
horn, cornū, -ūs, n. [XXIX]
hour, hōra, -ae, f. [XXVIII]
household, domus, -ūs, f. [XXIX]
huge, ingens, ingentis [XXXIII]
hurt, vulnerō (1) [I]

I

in front of, prō, (+ abl.) [XXIV]
in, in (+ abl.) [XXIV]
inhabitant, incola, -ae m. [XXII]
into, in, (+ acc.) [XVII]

J

javelin, tēlum, -ī, n. [XV]
journey, iter, itineris, n. [XXIII]

K

keen, ācer, ācris, ācre [XXV]
kill, interficiō, -ficere, -fēcī, -fectum [XVII]
king, rex, rēgis, m. [XXVII]
kingdom, regnum, -ī, n. [XXV]

L

land, terra, -ae, f. [XVI]
large, magnus, -a, -um [XII]
law, lex, lēgis, f. [XIX], iūs, iūris, n. [XXIII]
lead, dūcō, dūcere, dūxī, ductum [X]
leader, dux, ducis, m. [XIX]
letter, epistula, -ae, f. [V]
light, lūx, lūcis, f. [XXV]
like, amō (1) [I]
like, similis, -e [XXXI]
listen to, audiō (4) [XIV]
little, parvus, -a, -um [XII]
long, longus, -a, -um [XX]
love, amō (1) [I]
loyal, pius, -a, -um [XVIII]
loyalty, fidēs, -eī, f. [XXXII]

M

make, faciō, facere, fēcī, factum [XVI]
make a journey, iter facere [XVI]
make a mistake, errō (1) [II]

man, vir, virī, m. [IX]
many, multī, -ae, -a [XII]
march, iter facere [XVI]
master, dominus, -ī, m. [VIII]
matter, rēs, -eī, f. [XXXII]
messenger, nuntius, -ī, m. [XI]
mine, meus, -a, -um [XII]
misfortune, cāsus, -ūs, m. [XXIX]
mother, māter, mātris, f. [XXVI]
mountain, mons, montis, m. [XXV]
move, moveō, movēre, mōvī, mōtum [XXVII]
much, multus, -a, -um [XII]
my, meus, -a, -um [XII]

N

name, nōmen, nōminis, n. [XX]
nation, gens, gentis, f. [XXI]
native land, patria, -ae, f. [V]
next, proximus, -a, -um [XXVIII]
night, nox, noctis, f. [XXV]
not, nōn [I]

O

on, in (+ abl.) [XXIV]
onto, in, (+ acc.) [XVII]
our, noster, nostra, nostrum [XIII]
out of , ē, ex, (+ abl.) [XXIV]

P

perceive, cernō, cernere, crēvī, crētum [XXX]
pirate, pīrāta, -ae, m. [XXII]
place, pōnō, pōnere, posuī, positum [X]
plain, campus, -ī, m. [XV]
playing field, campus, -ī, m. [XV]
poet, poēta, -ae, m. [IV]
possessions, rēs, rērum, f. pl. [XXXII]
praise, laudō (1) [I]
prepare, parō (1) [III]
proceed, tendō, tendere, tetendī, tensum/tentum [XXXIII]
punish, pūniō (4) [XIV]
put, pōnō, pōnere, posuī, positum [X]

Q

queen, rēgīna, -ae, f. [IV]
quick, celer, celeris, celere [XXV]

R

receive, accipiō, accipere, accēpī, acceptum [XVII]
remain, maneō, manēre, mānsī, mānsum [XXIV]
report, nūntiō (1) [XXII]
right, iūs, iūris, n. [XXIII]
rim, ōra, -ae, f. [XVI]
rise, surgō, surgere, surrēxī, surrēctum [XXXIII]
river, flūmen, flūminis, n. [XX]
road, iter, itineris, n. [XXIII]
roll, volvō, volvere, volvī, volūtum [XXX]

rule, regō, regere, rēxī, rēctum [XXVIII]
run away, fugiō, fugere, fūgī, fugitum [XVI]

S

sad, tristis, -e [XXXIII]
sailor, nauta, -ae, m. [XXII]
say, dīcō, dīcere, dīxī, dictum [XXVIII]
sea, mare, maris, n. [XXI]; flūctūs, -uum, m. (pl.) [XXIX]
secretary, scrība, -ae, m. [XXII]
see, videō, vidēre, vīdī, vīsum [VII]
seize, capiō, capere, cēpī, captum [XVI]
send, mittō, mittere, mīsī, missum [X]
serious, gravis, -e [XXX]
set up, pōnō, pōnere, posuī, positum [X]
shadow, umbra, -ae, f. [VII]
sharp, ācer, ācris, ācre [XXV]
shelter, tegō, tegere, tēxī, tēctum [XXX]
ship, nāvis, nāvis, f. [XXI]
shore, ōra, -ae, f. [XVI]; lītus, lītoris, n. [XX]
short, brevis, -e [XXVI]
show, monstrō (1) [XXII]
sick, aeger, aegra, aegrum [XVII]
sight, speciēs, -ēī, f. [XXXII]
similar, similis, -e [XXXI]
sing, cantō (1) [II]
sister, soror, sorōris, f. [XIX]
sit, sedeō, sedēre, sēdī, sessum [XXIV]
slave, servus, -ī, m. [XV]
sleep, somnus, -ī, m. [XV]
small, parvus, -a, -um [XII]
soldier, mīles, mīlitis, m. [XIX]
son, filius, -ī, m. [XI]
song, carmen, carminis, n. [XX]
speak, dīcō, dīcere, dīxī, dictum [XXVIII]
stand, stō, stāre, stetī, stātum [XXIV]
stay, maneō, manēre, mānsī, mānsum [XXIV]
step, gradus, -ūs, m. [XXIX]
stretch out, tendō, tendere, tetendī, tensum/tentum [XXXIII]
stretch upward, surgō, surgere, surrēxī, surrēctum [XXXIII]
strong, fortis, -e [XXIX]
sweet, dulcis, -e [XXX]
swell, surgō, surgere, surrēxī, surrēctum [XXXIII]
swift, celer, celeris, celere [XXV]

T

take, capiō, capere, cēpī, captum [XVI]
tall, altus, -a, -um [XII]
task, opus, operis, n. [XX]
teach, doceō, docēre, docuī, doctum [VI]
teacher, magister, magistrī, m. [VIII]
tell, dīcō, dīcere, dīxī, dictum [XXVIII]
thing, rēs, -eī, f. [XXXII]
tired, fessus, -a, -um [XVIII]
to, ad (+ acc.) [XVII]
towards, ad (+ acc.) [XVII]
tribe, gēns, gentis, f. [XXI]

U

under, sub, (+ abl.) [XXIV]
unhappy, miser, misera, miserum [XIII]
useful, ūtilis, -e [XXXI]

V

vast, ingēns, ingentis [XXXIII]
voice, vōx, vōcis, f. [XIX]

W

wage, gerō, gerere, gessī, gestum [XXX]
wall, mūrus, -ī, m. [XV]
wander, errō (1) [II]
war, bellum, -ī, n. [XV]
warn, moneō (2) [VI]
watch over, servō (1) [III]
water, aqua, -ae, f. [V]
wave, flūctus, -ūs, m. [XXIX]
way, iter, itineris, n. [XXIII]
weapon, tēlum, -ī, n. [XV]
wicked, malus, -a, -um [XVIII]

wind, ventus, ī, m. [XV]
wise, sapiēns, sapientis [XXXIII]
with, cum, (+ abl.) [XXIV]
without, sine, (+ abl.) [XXIV]
woods, silva, -ae, f. [VII]
word, verbum, -ī, n. [IX]
work, opus, operis, n. [XX]
wound, vulnerō (1) [II]
wrath, īra, -ae, f. [VII]
wretched, miser, misera, miserum [XIII]
write, scrībō, scrībere, scrīpsī, scrīptum [X]
writer, scrība, -ae, m. [XXII]

Y

year, annus, -i, m. [XXVIII]
your, tuus, -a, -um (belonging to one person) [XII]; vester, vestra, vestrum (belonging to more than one person) [XIII]
yours, tuus, -a, -um (belonging to one person) [XII]; vester, vestra, vestrum (belonging to more than one person) [XIII]

INDEX